"Take it from me, as someone who has worked in both government and business: leadership matters! In the face of global challenges like the climate crisis and the Covid-19 pandemic, the need for good leaders in every part of society has never been greater. In *Leadership Reckoning*, the Doerr Institute for New Leaders pioneers a data-driven approach to make the development of moral leadership a core function of college education. This book is a must-read for the leaders of today and tomorrow."

—Al Gore, Former Vice President of the United States of America

"This book and the ongoing work at the Doerr Leadership Institute, along with its consortium of higher educational institutions, seeks to elevate the leadership development practice in higher education to be authentic. What I mean here is having all of us validate our aspirational statements about developing the next generation of leaders by demonstrating we have contributed our part in doing so. To be clear, this reckoning is by no means a simple task, but by presenting this challenge, the authors place the onus upon all of us to address it—a good place to start toward being authentic."

—Bruce J. Avolio, Mark Pigott Chair in Business Strategic Leadership at the Foster School of Business at the University of Washington

"*Leadership Reckoning* is providing the contextual framework and the directional compass for mastering the Fourth Industrial Revolution, with its complex and fast-paced change."

—Klaus Schwab, Founder and Executive Chairman of the World Economic Forum

"In *Leadership Reckoning: Can Higher Education Develop the Leaders We Need?*, Thomas Kolditz, Libby Gill, and Ryan Brown unveil all of the ways that colleges and universities are underserving our student leaders. The book is a call to action for anyone who has ever taught a leadership class or run a higher ed leader program. Most importantly, the book offers a step-by-step guide for educators to improve their leader development efforts by defining what they mean by leadership, using evidence-based practice rather than leader-tainment, and measuring actual leader outcomes"

—Stefanie K. Johnson, Academic Director of Center for Leadership and Associate Professor at the University of Colorado Boulder

"This book is a gem of a resource for institutions of higher education considering their role and approach in preparing the rising generation to exert the leadership our world needs. It is hard to imagine a more important question for revitalizing our colleges and universities and, most importantly, for getting on the path to realizing our collective aspirations for a just, sustainable, and peaceful world."

—Wendy Kopp, CEO and Co-founder of Teach for All

Leadership Reckoning challenges the status quo by putting forth a call to action and suggests bold strategies for institutions of higher education that are reconsidering traditional approaches to advancing leadership development."

—Justin Greenleaf, Immediate Past President of the Association of Leadership Educators

"Young people truly are the future of any country, and the degree to which they understand and embrace the keys to successful leadership has a profound effect not only on their future but also on that of their community and country. If ever there was a time for increased focus on what works in leadership training for young people in the U.S., now is it! Tom Kolditz, along with his Doerr Institute colleagues, brings a lifetime of experience in building leaders to this important book for young leaders."

—Carolyn Miles, Former CEO of Save the Children

"At long last, the whistle has been blown: the gap between commercial claims of producing leaders and the actuality of effective leader development in higher education is large and problematic. This is a promising, instructive book every educator needs to read if higher education is to take its rightful place in producing needed leaders for the future."

—Susan MacKenty Brady, CEO of Simmons University Institute for Inclusive Leadership

"Strong leadership is the foundation of any healthy organization or society. This book illustrates the important role that universities can play in leadership development. I could not think of a more important and timely book."

—Reginald DesRoches, Provost and Professor of Engineering at Rice University

"Our students will impact the world in a greater proportion than their numbers. Higher education needs to fulfill its promise to students and society to prepare them to lead in a complex and hyper-connected world. This book makes a compelling case for leadership being central to the university mission and, more importantly, delivering on that mission."

—Cynthia Cherrey, President and CEO of the
International Leadership Association

"Young people step into leadership positions much earlier than their colleagues from previous generations. But are they prepared? Leadership preparedness is what is desperately needed. What Rice University and the Doerr Institute, in particular, are doing with the help of professional coaching is a 'must-have' and should be embraced by all institutions of higher education. The future belongs to these young leaders, and they need to be leaders in the first place."

—Magdalena Nowicka Mook, CEO and Executive Director
of the International Coaching Federation (ICF)

"Universities must constantly critique their methods and find more effective ways to achieve their goals. The Doerr Institute for New Leaders at Rice University was envisioned boldly as leadership education available to ALL students, not just a select few. That required new ways of thinking about universities and leadership education. Tom Kolditz created an enterprise and ambition far different from other universities. In this important book, Tom and his coauthors set forth a new and empirically tested model, making the case for a transformation of university leadership education."

—David Leebron, President of Rice University

"Leadership is needed more than ever during these challenging times. The authors make the case that academia can play a critical role in leader development and, ultimately, have a positive impact across the entire spectrum of our society."

—Franklin Hagenbeck, Lieutenant General in the United States Army
and Director of the Engineering Leadership Institute
at the University of Florida

"Imagine every student at your institution having the opportunity to participate in developing their leadership skills formally. Imagine that those who participate come to see themselves as better leaders, perform more effectively as leaders, and do better in school than those who don't. Imagine no more. This is happening right now, and authors Tom Kolditz, Libby Gill, and Ryan Brown show you where and how in Leadership Reckoning. This book is at once a manifesto and a guide to fulfilling one of higher education's core missions—to develop the capacity of future leaders to serve their communities better."

—Jim Kouzes, Coauthor of the bestselling and award-winning book *The Leadership Challenge* and former Dean's Executive Fellow of Leadership at the Leavey School of Business at Santa Clara University

"This groundbreaking book highlights how colleges and universities can properly leverage social science in order to forge leader identity in their students."

—Bernard B. Banks, Associate Dean for Leadership Development and Inclusion at the Kellogg School of Management at Northwestern University

"Higher education institutions have an urgent obligation to develop real-world leadership skills in students, and the authors provide innovative, practical ways to accomplish that mission. This groundbreaking book is a must-read for every university administrator and board member."

—John R. Ryan, President and CEO of the Center for Creative Leadership and former Chancellor of the State University of New York

"Historically, the noble calling of educating an informed citizenry gave American higher education a position of great respect across the nation. As we have consistently failed to meet emerging challenges like access, equity, costs, and, most importantly, mission clarity, the grinding degradation of our reputation cries out for a bold solution. This book lays out beautifully how focusing on providing the nation's supply of leaders meets that call."

—Helen Drinan, President of Simmons University

"The team at the Doerr Institute for New Leaders at Rice has reimagined student leadership development in ways that are firmly grounded in evidence-based theory and practices. The book provides a clear and compelling blueprint for effectively developing young adults to be leaders for their times. It is an essential read."

—David V. Day, Academic Director and Professor of Psychology at the Kravis Leadership Institute at Claremont McKenna College

"*Leadership Reckoning* sets the gold standard for how to develop students as leaders. Tom Kolditz, Libby Gill, and Ryan Brown describe a strategic, systematic, and structured process of self-discovery and purposeful practice, supported by professional coaching and leadership training. Befitting the context of higher education, this unique approach is distinguished by its rigorous measurement of outcomes and evidence-based design. Given the current shortfall of student leader development in higher education, feeding the workplace leadership pipeline with confident and competent graduates is essential to our collective future, and there is no better place to start than to apply the lessons from Leadership Reckoning."

—Tae Moon Kouzes, Managing Director and Executive Coach at Kouzes and Associates and Fellow at the Doerr Institute for New Leaders at Rice University

"Leadership is a multiplier—good and bad; we've seen both. Growing more leaders, better leaders, ethical leaders is a sacred public purpose of our colleges and universities. They owe us that. And they desperately need a 'leadership reckoning'—an accounting of success, an honest measurement of inevitable failures, and a clear charted path to improvement. Tom Kolditz, Libby Gill, and Ryan Brown have done precisely that in *Leadership Reckoning*. It is a must-read field guide to an optimistic future for our country and the world."

—Ann and John Doerr

Leadership Reckoning

Leadership Reckoning

Can Higher Education Develop the Leaders We Need?

THOMAS KOLDITZ, PH.D.

LIBBY GILL

RYAN P. BROWN, PH.D.

MONOCLE
PRESS

Table of Contents

Tables

Figures

Foreword

By Jim Collins

We are at a very interesting moment in the historical evolution of how free society operates.

Nearly a century ago, one of my intellectual mentors, Peter Drucker, made a three-part argument about a fundamental shift in the cellular structure of free society. First, he observed that we were becoming a society of organizations. For free society to function and compete, we must have high-performing, self-governed organizations in every sector, not just in business, but equally in government and the social sectors. Without that, in Drucker's view, the only workable alternative is totalitarian tyranny. Second, high-performing organizations, in turn, depend directly on excellent management. Good management makes human strength productive; bad management squanders human capability and destroys people's spirit. Third, developing management capability would become as important to the working of society as law, medicine, education, or the sciences. Viewed in a larger lens, Drucker saw management as a liberal art, requiring not merely technique but deep wisdom and enlightened, humane practice.

Drucker proved prescient; organizations well-managed did, indeed, become the cellular structure of free society working at its best. I sometimes muse that all subsequent management literature for the 20th century can be distilled down to a single sentence: Drucker was right.

But I also suspect we might now be in the midst of an equally profound historical shift, a reordering of free society into a next-iteration cellular structure: from a society of organizations well-managed into a society of *networks well-led*.

In a network, power is generally diffused and rarely does any one individual have enough concentrated power to get things done by mere directive. Leading in a network is more akin to being an effective senator—one of a hundred—than leading as a CEO vested with the power of executive decision. Effectiveness will increasingly rest upon the rarified ability to truly lead. True leadership only exists if people follow when they would otherwise have the freedom to not follow.

In 2012 and 2013, I had the privilege to serve a two-year appointment as the Class of 1951 Chair for the Study of Leadership at the United States Military Academy at West Point. It is one of the world's greatest leadership development institutions, having been in the business of building leaders of character for more than two centuries.

One of the informal mantras at West Point that stayed with me is the notion that you're a leader at every level of your service, no matter what your formal rank. I also learned that the military stereotype of martinets simply ordering people around is almost entirely unfounded. The best military leaders use power with great discretion and mostly lead by example, by request, by showing the way. Leadership is not about invoking rank; leadership is about seeing clearly what must be done, taking action, and inspiring others to join you in throwing their energies' full force into the task.

In my time as the leadership chair at West Point, I learned an important lesson from Brigadier General Bernard (Bernie) Banks, who was the head of the Department of Behavioral Sciences and Leadership before he retired from active military service to become the associate dean for Leadership Development and Inclusion at Northwestern University's Kellogg School of Management. He told me that he would sometimes receive phone calls from representatives at various universities who wanted to come and learn from West Point about leadership. How does West Point develop students as leaders? He would respond to them with a simple question. "What kind of leaders do you want them to be? What kind of character do you want them to have?" Banks found that even some of the most elite universities did not have a clear answer.

Universities have an important opportunity. They're never going to be quite like the military academies, such as West Point or Annapolis, nor should they be. But universities can learn an essential lesson from the academies: leadership development is not an "add-on" patch that we stick onto young people while they get their "real" education. Leadership development *is* the real education.

And leadership development is not about helping young people cultivate an extroverted "leadership personality." Across decades of research into what makes great companies tick, my research team and I found that few great company builders led with an outsized charismatic personality, and on the flip side, charismatic personalities often played a devastatingly toxic role in leading companies to disaster. The central task in leadership development is not about burnishing surface behaviors; the central task is about developing strong inner character.

What if universities were to fully embrace the mission to develop young women and men to be highly capable leaders in a diffused-power world, whatever they end up doing in life? What if students graduated with a similar perspective—that the point of their education is not just to gain knowledge and a degree but to *become a certain kind of person*. Highly proficient in some domain, yes, but more than that. The kind of person who sees clearly what must be done and does not wait for permission from authority or peer-group approval to act. The kind of person who sees everything through a prism of core values and who strives to live up to those values in every aspect of work and life. The kind of person who never sees other people as merely an expedient means to one's own career success and who earns the trust and love of those they lead. The kind of person who, by virtue of personal humility and indomitable will in service to a cause larger than oneself, inspires others to help in the achievement of BHAGs (Big Hairy Audacious Goals) that stimulate progress.

That strikes me as a powerful model for effective leadership in the 21st century. It is a model that the authors of this book, and the Doerr Institute itself, represent. But this level of leadership requires tremendous skill. This book is about creating the capability within universities to produce graduates with such skills—well developed and at grand scale.

How, then, do we develop such leaders at scale? Business schools have already put some thought into this question. But as Tom Kolditz of the Doerr Institute points out, business schools across the country only graduate about 100,000 people each year, and probably fewer than 30,000 are intensively developed as leaders. By contrast, colleges and universities in the U.S. alone graduate over 2.2 million people each year. What if we could influence a large portion of those young people and help them develop their leadership skills in a meaningful way? How much of an impact might we have on creating the society Peter Drucker envisioned—one that is both more productive and more humane?

The idea, here, is to create a double flywheel effect. In the research for *Good to Great*, my team and I uncovered the flywheel principle.[1] In creating a good-to-great transformation, there's no single defining action, no grand program, no miracle moment. Rather, it feels like turning a giant, heavy flywheel. Pushing with great effort, you get the flywheel to complete one entire turn. You don't stop. You keep pushing. The flywheel moves a bit faster, then faster still, adding more momentum as the flywheel spins. Then at some point—breakthrough! The flywheel flies forward with almost unstoppable momentum. Each turn builds upon previous work as you make a series of good decisions, supremely well executed, that compound one upon another. All great companies harness the flywheel effect.

Later, in *Good to Great and the Social Sectors*, I observed how the flywheel principle also applies to social sector institutions.[2] But there is a big difference between business flywheels and social flywheels. For a business, you can focus primarily on the flywheel of your own corporation. For the social sectors, however, there are always at least *two* flywheels. There is the flywheel of your specific institution, *and* there is the flywheel of the overall cause your institution serves. For example, the Cleveland Clinic must build its own flywheel as a leading healthcare institution *and* simultaneously contribute to the overall flywheel of a healthcare ecosystem that serves the well-being of all people. Leadership development at universities can contribute to the institutional flywheel of each specific university, as its graduates add to the school's reputation by virtue of their increasing leadership impact in life and work. This, in turn, contributes to the overall flywheel of universities stimulating progress across all of society. The two flywheels should reinforce each other, thereby elevating society *and* the role and reputation of universities within our society.

The arguments put forth in this book suggest that we can achieve this kind of leadership momentum at scale and that we can do so with objective, quantitative, measureable impact. That is a bold claim, and bold claims always need to be examined carefully. That said, if it is truly possible to build large numbers of students into leaders through cost-effective means, then we have a compelling argument for optimism that we can yet create the best American century.

America is at an inflection point. The question is, what is the trajectory? Will America fall into decline and decay, as have other great nations in history? Or will it experience a burst of self-renewal, a rebirth that reframes the 20th century as just the warm-up for the spectacular progress and upward trajectory of the 21st? Part of the answer may lie in how well we build millions of young people into leaders of character and how well we deploy those leaders into every walk of life.

The ability to innovate at scale marked America's rise in the 20th century. But imagine if we are able to *develop leaders at scale* as one of our greatest and most enduring innovations. Leadership might be the most important raw material America can offer the world. And without it, we may wind up with precious little to offer at all.

Introduction

CASTING A VISION FOR
LEADER DEVELOPMENT

In 2007, John Doerr returned to Rice University, his alma mater, to deliver the keynote address at graduation. Unbeknownst to him or anyone else, this would prove to be an important moment.

John is an engineer by training, which would not surprise anyone who met him for the first time. He dresses like an engineer—simply and with little effort to impress anyone. When he enters a room, he doesn't immediately take over the space or dominate every conversation. He is soft-spoken and deliberate when he communicates. He asks questions of the people around him and seems to care about their answers.

This description is unlikely to match what comes to mind for most people when they hear the word "billionaire." Nonetheless, that word applies to John Doerr, who made his fortune in Silicon Valley as a venture capitalist investing in the likes of Intel, Google, and Amazon, among many other super-star tech companies. Along with his wife, Ann (another Rice graduate), John Doerr is also a philanthropist, and it is this dimension of his remarkable life that made that 2007 keynote address at Rice important.

During his visit to the university, John was paraded around from one important person to another, as university leaders showed off the campus and looked for opportunities to encourage this favored son to continue his history of generosity to the school. Part of the parade, of course, involved a visit with a group of students. This was not a random selection of young scholars solicited from the student union, of course. These were hand-picked students meant to impress and inspire. They were meant to be the poster-children to motivate munificence—paragons of virtue, curiosity, and creativity. The best of the best.

John was not exactly dazzled.

To be sure, these students were all very intelligent. John recalled years later: "These were all very smart, very technically proficient people. But I'd say of the 24, there were only a couple of them that I think exhibited 'leader DNA.' They were, in a word, inarticulate." Despite being book smart, the students did not strike him as having the skills necessary to enter the world of work as effective leaders.

Ironically, this meeting *did* end up inspiring John and Ann to give generously to Rice. They were inspired, more specifically, to endow a new initiative—later known as the Doerr Institute for New Leaders—with a primary mission of helping Rice students grow as leaders and assisting them in developing the non-academic skills they would need if they ever wanted to make a difference in the world as decision-makers, influencers, innovators, entrepreneurs, and scholars. Notably, the structure is a freestanding institute, not a center managed by a dean who is part of a specific school within the university. An institute functions with greater creative autonomy across all schools in a university and reports to senior leadership. This is a baseline consideration for university leader development.

But John and Ann's vision for the institute that bears their name extends beyond Rice to the wider world of higher education. They want to elevate the practice of leader development at all top institutions of higher education. They want to model and share effective practices and motivate other universities to make leader development the priority that these institutions often claim it is. Universities *can* get more serious about leader development without a billionaire to endow an institute, by the way. In fact, highly impactful leader development work can be executed at less cost per student than traditional classroom teaching can. This book describes one way that can be done, although with focus, vision, and commitment, there are certainly many ways that colleges and universities could pursue meaningful leader development on their campuses.

Yet, as we will describe in this book, most universities are seriously failing in this regard. While corporations and the military have embraced professional leader development strategies, even the best schools lag far behind and rarely achieve a level of quality in their programs that is on par with their academic teaching and training. Indeed, much of what passes for leader development in universities is little more than a collection of titillating and mildly inspiring moments that we like to refer to as "leader-tainment"— motivational speakers, field trips, afternoon teas with the dean, and the occasional ropes course—none of which would qualify as actual leader development anywhere else. In the best case, what's supposed to build leadership abilities is more often focused on professional or career development, such as training on how to interview well or how to network effectively.

If universities were honest about offering little more than such entertaining moments, students would know what they were and were not getting as part of their degrees and simply plan to obtain actual leadership training beyond the ivory tower. The reality is, though, that most colleges advertise through their mission statements and marketing materials that they do, actually, produce leaders. We would argue that such assertions, even from top-tier universities, are well intended but empty promises. The problem, we think, can be traced back to several factors:

- Universities do not typically use evidence-based leader development strategies (if they have an articulated strategy at all). It is somewhat ironic that universities have not kept pace with the science of leader development, given that much of this science comes from universities in the first place.
- Universities do not employ professional leader developers but, instead, rely on well-meaning faculty or staff with little to no expertise in the realm of leader development. If you wouldn't go to an untrained doctor for a nose job or an untrained dentist for a root canal, why would you go to an untrained volunteer to help students develop leadership skills?
- The approach that universities often take to leader development is, at its root, more about developing professional/academic excellence than about developing leadership skills. Just because a school produces excellent chemists doesn't mean that those technically competent chemists know how to lead others, in a lab or elsewhere.
- Universities rarely measure the outcomes of their efforts to develop students as leaders (aside from popularity or participation measures). Thus, if they did happen to being doing something that helped students grow their leadership capacity, no one would know it, nor would anyone know which initiatives were a waste of time and money.

Our research shows that people frequently assume that graduating from a college or university would naturally produce growth in the ability to lead. In the fall of 2019, we hired a company that manages large, representative panels of Americans to administer a survey to over 200 college-educated adults from across the United States. The purpose of the survey was to discover what Americans tend to think about the role of higher education in producing leaders. The results were simple but instructive. Specifically, a majority (62 percent) believed that "students typically acquire the skills to lead during their time at university," and 67 percent likewise believed that "universities do a good job of preparing students for leadership." In contrast to such beliefs, however, our research at Rice University shows that, on average, students exhibit virtually no measurable growth in leadership capacity across their four-year college experience, apart from engagement with formal leadership training. We will have more to say about our evidence for this disappointing lack of development later, in Chapter 1.

This disconnect between expectations and reality is in danger of undermining people's confidence in our institutions of higher education. If you've been led to believe that you'll graduate from a college or university with greater leadership capabilities but instead find that you have no more knowledge or confidence in leading than you had when you began, you might feel that you have been deceived (even if unintentionally) as you start the long process of repaying your college loans. Do universities recognize that there may be long-term consequences if people feel under served after spending enormous sums of money for their degrees? It's probably also worth noting that in our survey of American adults, we found that almost 70 percent felt strongly that developing students as leaders should be a core function of every college or university.

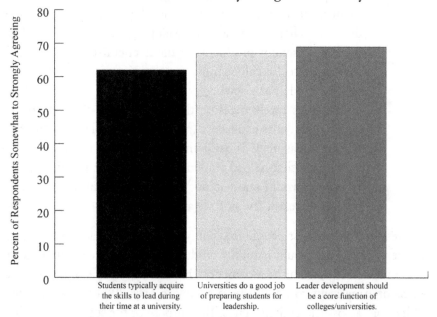

Figure 1. Results from a national survey of college-educated American adults (% of respondents *somewhat* to *strongly* agreeing with each statement)

According to the 2018 Edelman Trust Barometer,[3] a majority of Americans maintain trust in the military, small businesses, and the police "to do what is right," but trust in corporations, news media, and the government has dropped steeply. Only one-third of Americans say they trust their government, down 14 percentage points from the prior year. Under half (42 percent) trust the media, and though trust in business was slightly higher than trust in government or media, it also dropped 10 percentage points from 2017. Edelman also notes that, of all the world markets, the U.S. experienced the largest drop in trust in 2018, when it plummeted 37 points across all institutions. The Pew Research Center announced similar findings in a 2017 article that showed that, while American trust in military and scientists is relatively high, their trust in elected officials, business leaders, or media to act in the public's best interest is low.[4]

This pervasive lack of trust in institutions translates into a similar lack of faith in leaders. Indeed, Edelman's data spell out plainly what *Harvard Business Review* describes as "a staggering lack of confidence in leadership."[5] Specifically, 63 percent of respondents doubted the credibility of CEOs, and 71 percent doubted the credibility of government officials. Yet despite a clear and growing lack of trust in leadership, Edelman's Trust Barometer also found that Americans have high ideals for leaders, which is exemplified by the fact that nearly two-thirds (64 percent) believe that CEOs should "take the lead on change rather than waiting for government to impose it," and nearly 70 percent believe that the C-suite's number-one job should be building trust in their company.[6]

As just one example of what can happen when people stop trusting leaders and institutions, consider what might occur during an epidemic if people don't believe what scientists tell them about a particular disease or aren't willing to take the necessary measures to prevent a widespread outbreak. This is precisely what is happening in the U.S. and other Western countries with respect to vaccines. Because of public suspicion about the safety of vaccines, despite assurances by the medical community of their safety and efficacy, the U.S. and other countries are beginning to see a resurgence of infectious diseases that were thought to be nearly eradicated, such as the measles.[7] Likewise, the novel coronavirus, SARS-CoV-2, is ravaging the country and the world as we write this book, and an effective vaccine for the associated COVID-19 disease has yet to be created. But a survey conducted in May of 2020 showed that, even if an effective vaccine was available, only 49 percent of Americans would avail themselves of it.[8] If half of the public sees misconduct by medical researchers or doctors as at least a moderately big problem,[9] is it any wonder that false information can spread via the internet to "infect" the populace and change public behavior? In the absence of trustworthy leaders, false prophets will always rise to fill the void.

It would be easy to go on about the crisis of trust in our nation's institutions and leaders, lament its negative impact on our culture, and debate how we got here. Yet at this juncture, the rear-view is of little use; the question that's more relevant is, what are we going to do now to boost trust in the next generation of leaders? Creating leaders who can address such trust deficits starts with our institutions of higher education.

Ann Doerr, a Rice engineering alum like her husband and board chair of the Khan Academy, recently discussed the Doerr Institute's goal to train students to become effective leaders. She stated, "A true leader needs the skills to evaluate the goal, understand its validity, succinctly articulate it, and then lead with deep compassion, moral integrity, and empathy."[10] Yet how can universities generate great leaders that match these descriptions? Such leaders are *made*, not born. They need to be trained to recognize and build on their strengths while continuously self-correcting to overcome deficits. They need guidance concerning which tools to use in order to achieve different leadership goals, and they need the self-awareness to know when to use them.

At the Doerr Institute, we have begun to address these needs by offering developmental opportunities to every Rice student who is interested in growing as a leader. To be certain, we have encountered far more questions than we've had answers to when it comes to the essential ingredients for building an effective leader development program. And while we believe that we are doing transformational work, we're not claiming to have the final word on leader development. Indeed, what we've done well has largely been the result of adapting discoveries made by other academics and leadership experts, which we will reference throughout the book. Nonetheless, we believe that progress in leader development is possible for anyone willing to take this work seriously and to apply a few "professionalizing principles" to their efforts. (We will talk more about our own version of such principles later.) We still have a great deal to learn, but we stand ready to share our experiences—our mistakes and missteps, as well as our successes—in the hope that others may benefit.

In our work creating the Institute and its programs, we have generally avoided one-size-fits-all leadership training models and, instead, created more individualized programs to help students become the leaders they desire to be. One of the benefits of this type of approach is that it helps students take responsibility for their own growth as leaders. In the long run, this might prove to be one of the most important aspects of our method. If students acquire some basic skills and a language for thinking about those skills, grow in self-awareness, and cultivate a sense of responsibility for their own development, then they will be positioned to continue enhancing their skills as leaders over time. That means that they will not only be a few steps ahead of their peers by the time they graduate, but they will also be on a different trajectory than their peers. It means that beyond the handful of semesters we have to work with them, they will have years to continue along this path of personal growth.

This book will describe not only what we see as the core problems in leader development among institutions of higher learning but also what we think are some of the solutions to these problems. In principle, we believe that colleges and universities that take leader development work seriously should (1) view (and treat) leader development as a core function of their institutions, (2) use evidence-based practices, (3) employ professional leader developers, and (4) measure the outcomes of their efforts rigorously, objectively, and continuously so that they know when they are succeeding and when they are not. We believe that if universities follow these broad principles, they cannot fail to improve as leader developers. At present, however, few colleges and universities (outside of the national service academies, arguably) appear to be following anything like these four principles.

Our mission at the Doerr Institute is not only to elevate the leadership capacity of Rice students but also to elevate the practice of leader development in higher education more broadly. To this end, we operate as an open collaborative that gives away everything we learn about developing students to other institutions. This book is just one example of how we do so. We hope that readers find it a useful guide as they consider how they, too, can take a more serious approach to this noble goal of developing leaders during what writer Meg Jay has termed "the defining decade" of students' lives, a period of critical development and great opportunity.[11] Although we begin this book with a critique, we are not cynical, and our perspective is much more hopeful than the next chapter might suggest. We know that institutions of higher learning *can* do a better job developing the leadership abilities of students. Because the world desperately needs great leaders to solve the immense social and environmental problems it faces, we *must* do better.

Chapter 1

GRADUATING LEADERS?

Leader-tainment and the Claims of Higher Education

Several years ago, one of the authors of this book adopted a dog from a local shelter that specialized in rescuing boxers that had been abandoned by their owners. The author was traveling frequently, and a dog seemed like a good way to protect his family in his absence. As a breed, boxers are not only loyal companions and very good with young children, but their strength and fierce countenance also make them look like animals that an intruder would not take lightly. Those qualities seemed like the perfect combination in a guard dog. The family named their newest member Penny, after her copper-colored coat.

In a remarkably unlikely occurrence, this perception was actually put to the test early one morning when an intruder entered the author's home as most of his family slept. A crucial feature of this intruder was that he was covered in blood (his own blood, we should note, not that of a hapless victim of any prior misdeeds). That fact alone should have alerted Penny to his presence. But it didn't. When the author realized that someone was in the house who was not supposed to be there, he noted that Penny had never barked or pointed the way. She merely wagged her stump of a tail and followed him merrily as he searched the home. She didn't attack the intruder or growl menacingly when he was eventually located, and she seemed almost disappointed when the strange, blood-soaked man was ejected from the house without getting to pet her. In short, Penny was an absolutely useless guard dog.

We relate this story to make a simple point. Penny was supposed to serve as a deterrent to anyone who might be up to no good, and if that failed, she was supposed to go on the attack. She was the right breed for this role, and she certainly looked the part. Unfortunately, as it turns out, having the right pedigree and looking the part are not enough. Penny had never been trained to be a guard dog, so in this critical moment, she didn't know how to do what she was expected to do.

For us, Penny seems a fitting metaphor for how leader development tends to work—or not work—within colleges and universities in the United States. We will explain what we mean throughout this chapter, and we will make the case here and in subsequent chapters that not only *can* we do better but also that we *must* do better. Having a good institutional pedigree and looking the part are not enough for colleges and universities, any more than they were for Penny.

Common Claims Among Colleges and Universities

It's commonplace for universities in the United States to claim that developing the next generation of leaders is central to their mission. For instance, Yale University's website, on a page titled "What Yale Looks For," notes, "We are looking for students we can help to become the leaders of their generation in whatever they wish to pursue."[12] Similarly, the mission of Rice University is to "produce leaders across the spectrum of human endeavor."[13] Such mission statements are common, particularly among the most selective, elite universities in the country. Everyone seems to be all about developing leaders.

If we look more closely at these claims, it's clear that most schools actually have no idea whether, or to what extent, they are developing students as leaders. The gap between this claim and reality means that schools are misleading students, parents, donors, and the public about what they really provide in this critical arena. The misrepresentation might come in the form of generic claims to "help prepare leaders for tomorrow" via fundraising emails or through the offer of random activities labeled as "leadership training" to students, such as ropes courses, trust falls, or teas held in residence halls with VIPs and school administrators—exercises that are essentially meaningless when it comes to measurably building skills that today's leaders need. Exaggerations regarding the scope and scale of leadership training are reflected in the frequent tendency of schools to offer small programs that are available only to a tiny group of handpicked students holding certain majors or participating in specific activities (often those who already self-identify as leaders, rather than those who wish to develop their leadership skills).

No matter how these grand claims are delivered, one commonality is clear: the same institutions that loudly proclaim their success in leader development rarely articulate, even loosely, what student leadership development on their campuses involves, nor do they tend to invest in careful measurement of the outcomes of their programs to determine whether or not they are, in fact, increasing students' capacity to lead. Students certainly suffer from this deficit; they jump in with good faith only to emerge disappointed. One junior at Rice University described a popular leadership conference she attended that was put on by another university—a university that appears in at least one top-10 list for student leadership programs and was identified as one of the top schools in our own preliminary research on university programs. By way of background, this student had already participanted in every program that the Doerr Institute had offered at Rice. This was a student who cared about her own development as a leader and was enthusiastic about new experiences that promised to help her grow.

Her experience at this leadership conference was, to say the least, underwhelming. After spending three-and-a-half hours drawing nametags, playing Two Truths and a Lie, answering 20 Questions with a ball of yarn, and spending upward of 30 minutes deciding on a karaoke song for the final night, the student said she felt confused as to why she was there. As a result, she decided to leave this highly regarded conference early.

The student later explained to us that the group workshops at this conference were "just lectures with poorly guided activity and discussion." For example, an instructor delivered a 30-minute PowerPoint of general leadership truisms, such as "a good leader also has to know how to be a follower." Rather than showing students how the content of the workshop could help them become better leaders, the broad assertions made by the instructor were thrown out to the audience with no hint of personal applications or suggested mechanisms for skill development. "We just made a poster of our strengths as the activity and went around and shared one of the featured strengths," she noted. "When I was ready to participate, my group leader had already changed the topic to something else." She concluded that the lack of actual skill development opportunities, fuzzy content, and emphasis on adolescent-oriented activities led her to feel like she was at a "weekend summer camp with a poorly executed focus on leadership" rather than a professional leadership development conference at a collegiate level.

While this student's feedback is based on her personal experience at an event billed as a leadership conference rather than a formal program at a university, the feedback is nonetheless telling. Such "leader-tainment" events often serve as the central components—if not the sole components—of many university leader development programs. The types of "fluffy" activities and approaches to grooming young leaders that this student describes encountering at the conference largely mirror what our research found is happening in such programs more broadly. We use the term "leader-tainment" to characterize activities that are sold as leader development but amount to little more than a few laughs and feel-good moments. That's the type of program that our research found predominates the current leader development landscape in U.S. colleges and universities.

Students aren't the only victims of such flimsy leader training. Faculty members, likewise, suffer from their own insufficient personal development and an insipid institutional investment in the development of students. This creates a vicious cycle in which a university's failure to support its staff in helping students grow as leaders causes attrition among faculty who take this kind of work seriously, which results in even less support for effective student programming among those who remain. As one leadership development professional from a top-tier, East Coast business school explained, confidentially, to us:

> One of the reasons I left my position in the business school was the lack of resources and faculty support for pushing the envelope in leader development in the MBA program. When I had to raise my own money ($60,000+ in two years) to make things work, I decided it was enough.

Bear in mind that this quote comes from a faculty member in a business school—the place where some of the only strategic investments in leader development tend to be made in universities.

The Reality of Leader Development in Higher Education

These individual stories appear illustrative of a larger pattern when viewed in the context of more systematic research into these programs. To help illuminate the overarching problem, we conducted our own investigation to evaluate the state of student leadership development in universities across the United States. As part of our research, we interviewed key personnel at 56 universities that either self-identified or were identified by independent sources (e.g., "best colleges" rankings) as valuing student leadership development. The purpose of our interviews was to address the following questions:

- What leadership development opportunities—and how many—are currently offered at the institution (e.g., student advisory councils, leadership competency workshops, community engagement projects, professional one-on-one coaching)?
- How centrally organized and managed are the leadership opportunities that are offered? Are most or all student leadership opportunities provided through a single campus entity or are they scattered across different departments/offices throughout the university?
- To whom are these developmental opportunities made available? Are they offered only to a limited number of students, such as students in a certain major, or are they offered to everyone without limitation?
- What is the level of training or expertise in leader development among instructors or facilitators? Are they student leaders, untrained mentors, well-meaning alumni, professional coaches?
- Do the outcomes of these programs ever get measured? Do trained researchers administer tests of leadership capacity before and after developmental experiences, record structured observations of leadership skills, analyze ratings made by acquaintances, or track any leadership-related outcomes following graduation? If so, do such data get used to change the nature or delivery of any programs?

We began our investigation by contacting universities identified in *College Magazine*'s "10 Best Schools For Future Leaders"[14] and *U.S. News & World Report*'s national "Best Colleges Rankings" of the Top 25 national universities.[15] We contacted additional universities based on top hits from internet searches using key terms such as "student leaders," "student leadership development," and "university leadership development." Given that few universities have any centralized management for leadership education and development, the representatives with whom we spoke were often staff or faculty in charge of a prominent program who also felt comfortable describing other leadership initiatives across the university.

While our sample was admittedly limited to the schools that agreed to participate in interviews and, thus, is not necessarily representative of all U.S. universities, it's notable that our sample did include many Ivy League schools and other top-tier institutions that are often identified as—and typically proclaim to be—the "leaders" in creating leaders.

Our interviews revealed several key trends:

- Leadership development opportunities in U.S. universities are often available to only a select group of students who typically are from specific academic disciplines (e.g., business majors, engineers) and who must compete for the opportunities.
- These development opportunities are often scattered around campus and are not under the umbrella or direction of any single entity or office that serves the entire campus. Consequently, they lack developmental coherence and organizational integrity and are usually inadequately funded compared to other endeavors like classroom teaching.
- Most of the leadership opportunities are either geared toward—or are limited to—only undergraduate students, with minimal or no graduate student presence outside of MBA programs.
- Most programs do not employ professional leader developers; many, in fact, are student facilitated, with the exception of a few that are staff-led. (Although even in these cases, it is not always clear that the staff involved have any professional training in leader development.)
- Measurement of the impact of these programs is either nonexistent or is limited to students' self-reported satisfaction or participation levels. These limitations arguably render any formal rankings of such programs virtually meaningless (yet another problem that needs to be addressed in a reformation of higher education's leader development "enterprise").

We can summarize our findings by acknowledging that U.S. universities, by and large, do not use evidence-based leader development strategies, and many appear to have no coherent strategy in this regard whatsoever. When leader development programs do exist, they are commonly offered only to an elite handful of students in specific groups who may be required to compete for entry and sometimes even have to pay for the privilege.

Limiting opportunities for students to obtain leadership development rather than offering it to the whole student body reinforces the view that leadership is not for everyone but is, instead, reserved for a privileged few—a narrative that supports universities underfunding leader development while nonetheless claiming excellence as leader developers.

This elitism mirrors the common approach in industry of offering leadership training only to employees who are identified as "high potentials" rather than to all employees. Considering that those who complete a college degree in general—not to mention doing so at a highly selective university—have already been pre-selected for having demonstrated "high potential," why wouldn't we treat *every* college student as being capable of growing as a leader? To put a finer point on the matter, who is letting all of these "low potential" students into our colleges and universities, and why haven't they been fired yet?

Adding insult to injury, we can clearly see that what's promoted in university marketing materials is not, in fact, what is actually being offered to students, given that so many top-tier schools seem to routinely inflate claims about the comprehensiveness of their programs, the access to trained leadership professionals, and the empirically validated outcomes students will experience. Some examples that interviewees in our study shared about the types of leader development opportunities on their campuses include:

- Local business leaders coming in to chat with students or deliver speeches about their leadership style or experiences;
- One-off student conferences with no articulated goals or follow-up plans that are typically offered to only a small group of students;
- Student clubs that offer no mechanisms for feedback or formal training;
- Leadership research and theory courses with no measured developmental goals or outcomes;
- Internal presentations held within "leadership centers" and given by faculty known only to a small group of other faculty members;
- Ropes courses, residence hall teas, or other such social gimmicks.

Consider the case of the typical, high-status leadership speaker. Such speakers often garner fees of $50K or more, depending on their degree of national prominence and the level of demand for their time. While there might well be some general educational value to be gained from listening to such prominent individuals talk, the implicit assumptions behind such events appears to be that, in the aftermath of being spoken to, students will remember what the speaker said, consider its relevance for their own lives, find it persuasive enough to motivate them to change their minds or habits, develop a set of personal goals related to what they heard, and actively pursue those goals on their own. In other words, U.S. colleges and universities pay a lot of money to have "leadership experts" talk at students and, presumably, believe that change will come merely from hearing these gurus' words of wisdom. How likely is that to occur? And more importantly, is there any evidence—any empirical, quantifiable data at all—that such change is common?

We find these assumptions to be unwarranted and somewhat naïve. Such a passive receipt of ideas on its own is unlikely to cause substantial shifts in anyone's behavioral, cognitive, or emotional skills to an extent that it improves his or her ability to lead. The same goes for listening to one-off webinars, attending classes on the history of leaders or on leadership theory, or taking leadership-themed tours of battlefields like Gettysburg or Omaha Beach. (Those are not random examples, by the way—they come from our interviews with leader developers.) Inspiring? Perhaps. Interesting? Sometimes. But can a speaker magically morph students into better leaders just by talking to them? We would argue that assuming this to be true gets in the way of understanding and delivering far more impactful interventions. If this approach were really sufficient, then we could just have students watch TED talks or listen to some carefully curated podcasts and call it a day. Mission accomplished.

Our investigation also revealed another common characteristic of leader development in many top-tier universities: when you scratch beneath the surface, it becomes clear that what's being promoted as leadership training actually amounts to career-building or developing professional competencies in a specific discipline, as opposed to honing leadership skills that can help people lead across any type of organization or industry. Without careful attention to the differentiation between leader development and other equally worthy aims, the latter can easily displace the former. We ought to closely inspect the accuracy of any claims made by a college or university about leader development, which by definition means increasing a person's ability or capacity to lead, to ensure that such claims don't actually refer to some other kind of development. Additionally, although formal programs might profess to build leadership capacity, simply providing opportunities for students to serve in a leadership role using their existing skill set isn't the same as training them to lead well. Analogously, would we call someone a mechanic just because they had been given the opportunity to tinker with car engines on their own? Does having a little grease on your hands credential you as being ready to fix someone's car? Would you ever let someone like this work on *your* car?

Yet universities frequently make such claims, in part, because students, parents, and donors care deeply about an institution's reputation when it comes to leader development.[16] The high value placed on proclamations about the quality of a university's leadership training is evidenced by the popularity of rankings like those published by *U.S. News & World Report*[17] and *College Magazine*,[18] even though, as we have argued, these rankings might well constitute an additional layer of misleading information when we consider schools' actual leadership offerings and lack of measurable outcomes. As John Byrne (former editor-in-chief of *Fast Company* and executive editor of *Business Week*) wrote about such ranking systems, "It's a monster effort, and it draws monster attention, both from anxious parents and students who are about to make major investments in higher education and from the many critics who view these rankings as something of a farce."[19]

Why do college presidents reportedly "bemoan the list" each year? Because, as Byrne continues, "They point out that the ranking depends heavily on unaudited, self-reported data that encourages cheating and harmful admission practices." Indeed, during the writing of this very chapter, one prominent, public university was removed from *U.S. News & World Report*'s college rankings upon the discovery that the school had been falsifying data on alumni giving (a key metric in the magazine's ranking system) for nearly 20 years.[20] This school admitted fault in the matter and, in fact, brought the inaccuracy to the attention of *U.S. News & World Report* in the first place. Nonetheless, the example illustrates the broad problem that Byrne describes.

Byrne legitimizes the academic hand-wringing that accompanies publication of such rankings every year with some facts about what's really behind the methodology of this particular college ranking system and others like it:

> The problem with *U.S. News'* ranking and every other ranking of education, of course, is that determinations of "quality" turn on relatively arbitrary judgments about how each of these 16 different and imperfect variables collected by the publication should be weighted. As writer and bestselling author Malcolm Gladwell once pointed out in a scathing critique of *U.S. News'* rankings in the *New Yorker*, "There's no direct way to measure the quality of an institution—how well a college manages to inform, inspire, and challenge its students. So the *U.S. News* algorithm relies instead on proxies for quality—and the proxies for educational quality turn out to be flimsy at best."

U.S. News' sub-rankings, such as their ranking of "best undergraduate business programs," are even more suspect, according to Byrne, who highlights that the sub-rankings "are based on a single, highly questionable metric: a survey sent to deans and senior faculty members, rather than anything related to admissions standards, student experiences, or post-graduation outcomes." The dubious nature of these results, however, does little to dampen the near fanaticism with which the rankings are consulted. "[E]very year, millions of readers eat them up, giving *U.S. News'* powerful franchise in higher education more influence than ever before over application volume, alumni fund giving, and even faculty retirement," writes Byrne. He concludes that the whole ranking system amounts to little more than a "popularity contest that tends to reward the schools and programs that are generally regarded as best by academics—not students, alumni, or the companies that recruit from those schools." This is not a very compelling reason for students and their supporters to choose a school that's either touted as—or touts itself based on such lists as—one of the "best" for developing future leaders.

A Critical Period for Strategic Leader Development

We have argued that much of what is billed as leader development in U.S. colleges and universities isn't likely to result in any meaningful changes in students' abilities to lead. If we are right in this claim, the failure of higher education is magnified by the loss of this strategic time period—the life stage when most potentially impactful leader development work occurs (for the few who are lucky enough to be invested in as leaders). We would further argue that to be most effective, leader development needs to begin early, while people are still in a life stage that's biologically and culturally primed for learning. The college years are a particularly beneficial time for leadership growth, when personal identity is in greatest flux, even more so than during adolescence.[21] This period, sometimes referred to as "emerging adulthood" by developmental psychologists,[22] continues a trend of heightened risk-taking and experimentation that begins in adolescence but diminishes soon after. Indeed, as Stanford neuroscientist Robert Sapolsky has noted, the brain's preferences for food, music, and other types of basic sensory input are largely established by the late 20s, a pattern that is also exhibited in parallel form among non-human animals.[23] Because their habits of thought and behavior are not as deeply entrenched as those of a 45-year-old executive, emerging adults are more open and flexible in their thinking during this period. This gives young adults a greater capacity to develop social and emotional skills. It also complements their enhanced memory ability and cognitive processing speed,[24] precisely the skills that allow them to learn faster than older adults (and some of the basic building blocks of becoming capable leaders).

Another example of the strategic growth potential of young adults is seen through the Big Five Inventory (or BFI), a psychological scale that measures five basic dimensions of personality: extraversion, agreeableness, conscientiousness, neuroticism, and openness to experience.[25] The personality dimensions measured by the BFI are often associated with key leadership traits, including assertiveness, enthusiasm, and creative problem-solving.[26] The rate of change in these fundamental aspects of personality appears to be at its peak when people are between the ages of 18 and 25, followed by a leveling-off period and then a slight decline in the rate of change in later adulthood. Beyond age 40, almost no significant growth tends to appear in these aspects of personality. Thus, this period of emerging adulthood is a strategic time for investing in the cultivation of leadership skills.[27]

Science supports the wisdom of grooming leaders in college, during this unique window of time[28] when their brains are deciding which neural pathways to keep or discard, before their neuroplasticity diminishes and while their openness and identity are still in flux.[29] Yet that's not the way leaders are generally trained today. A common corporate strategy is to defer early-career leadership training and focus leadership resources on those who are already well-entrenched in their careers—those identified as "high-potential" employees. This reinforces an old and debunked stereotype (the "great man" theory) that leadership ability is an inborn characteristic to be identified in a select group, rather than a skill that can be learned by and cultivated in everyone.[30] Even worse, corporate leader development is often provided only after an employee is placed in a position of authority, usually because of his or her technical skills rather than because of the ability, or even inclination, to lead. Having great technical competencies in a particular field does not translate into being an effective leader, however, which is why executive coaches and trainers are often brought in to help close the gap between leaders' technical skills and their social-emotional skills. This creates an ongoing exercise of wait-and-catch-up. Is it any wonder that corporations in the U.S. alone spend upward of $14 billion every year on leader development efforts?[31]

How transformational would it be for institutions of higher education to intervene earlier in people's lives, to lay the foundations of key leadership competencies in their early 20s rather than waiting until their 40s or 50s? What benefits might accrue and accumulate over time if such investments were made early on in the life of a young leader? And how much more meaningful would academic institutions be if they were to move from merely claiming "we make leaders" in their recruitment materials to implementing evidence-based strategies for developing students as leaders in a thoughtful, coherent, and strategic way?

What Do the Data Say about the Natural Course of Leader Development?

With tuitions skyrocketing and young people often carrying debt for years to come, we consider it highly problematic for universities to claim that they offer powerful leader development opportunities when what they actually provide amounts to little more than leader-tainment. It's equally irresponsible of media outlets to highlight these programs as delivering quality leadership training when there is little or no evidence that they actually do so.

At this point, it is probably worth stepping back and taking a critical look at our arguments. Perhaps colleges and universities need not do anything more than they are already doing to develop students as leaders. Perhaps, in reality, giving students world-class professors in chemistry, philosophy, and literature is sufficient to enable them to develop leadership skills. Or, perhaps students will develop as leaders simply with time and maturity, and we needn't do anything comprehensive, coherent, or systematic to help them. We just need to make sure they are fed and sheltered and then get out of their way. Perhaps. But is there any evidence that students do, in fact, grow as leaders all by themselves while in school?

We took the liberty of asking this question at our own institution, which offers world-class professors to a highly select group of students, along with the regular cadre of leadership speakers, lunch-and-learn series, and the like. As one outcome measure, we examined students' leader identities, using data from a campus-wide survey of all Rice undergraduates in the fall of 2017.[32] Although leader identity can't be cultivated simply by reading about theories of leadership in the classroom, it *can* be measured. Indeed, there are several prominent leader identity measures that can be found in the academic literature, but they tend to focus on only one aspect of identity (most often self-categorization as a leader—in other words, the extent to which people see themselves as leaders).*[33] Because we view identity as being more complex and rich than just self-categorization, at the Doerr Institute we use a leader identity measure that includes self-categorization as a leader, self-confidence as a leader, willingness to lead, and self-awareness of one's strengths and weaknesses as a leader.[34] This assessment asks students to rate their level of agreement, on a scale from 1 to 5, with a series of statements, including (but not limited to) the following:

1. I see myself as a leader.
2. I feel confident to lead when opportunities arise.
3. I have a desire to pursue roles in which I can be a leader.
4. I have a clear understanding of my strengths as a leader.†

---

* Probably the most often cited leader identity measure in the academic research literature is a simple, 4-item measure (the "descriptive" dimension of leadership self-identity) that comes from a dissertation by Nathan Hiller, a student of acclaimed leadership researcher David Day, who we cite several times in this book.
† This measure, called the authentic leader identity scale, is described in more detail in Brown and Varghese (2019). In addition to self-categorization as a leader, items capture respondents' sense of self-confidence in their ability to lead, motivation to lead, awareness of their strengths and limitations as leaders, and tendencies to exhibit leadership in social situations. Briefly, in a sample of more than 2,800 students, this 9-item scale exhibited strong internal reliability ($\alpha = .89$) and a largely unitary factor structure. Over almost a full semester, scores on this measure also exhibited good test-retest reliability in a sample of 91 university students ($r = .70, p < .001$).

When we administered this leader identity measure to more than 2,800 Rice University undergraduates, the results were not encouraging. Rather than revealing a pattern of steady growth in leader identity over time, the data were essentially flat over four years. As shown in the graph below, freshmen exhibited strikingly similar leader identities as did seniors, which suggests that students were typically no better as leaders when they left the university than they were when they arrived from high school.

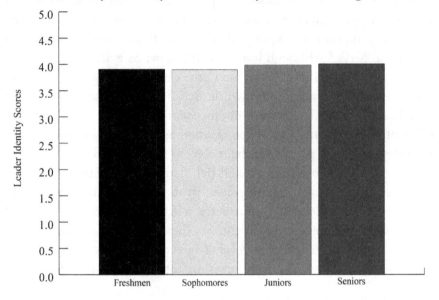

Figure 2. "Natural" trajectory of leader identity over time

Of course, students might have been wrong in this regard. Perhaps they actually had developed strong leadership skills over their four years of elite education. But if someone tells you he or she does not feel capable of cooking an edible meal, why would you make them a chef in an expensive restaurant? If college seniors are no more likely than freshmen to say that they see themselves as leaders, have confidence to lead, or are even willing to lead, why would we *not* believe them? Might it be because denying what they tell us in this matter serves our own purposes?

Another important question is whether leadership is really something that can be taught at all. If not, then universities are off the hook, right? Why would we ask schools to develop students in a domain in which there is really nothing that *can* be done, if some people are simply born to be great leaders, and everyone else just needs to understand that and follow them? Research has addressed this question, fortunately, and the evidence shows that although genes appear to play a role in who becomes a leader, just as they do in the realm of basic personality, most of the variability in leadership attainment (around 70 percent, in fact) seems to be due to experiential determinants, such as having the opportunity to practice one's leadership skills or receiving formal training and development.[35] But what kind of developmental intervention makes the most sense? How do universities avoid succumbing to the over-traveled road of feel-good moments and trust falls and, instead, offer students leader development experiences with true value?

Barriers to Progress in Higher Education

If we want to understand the influences that underlie the current shortfall in effective leader development in U.S. universities, one piece of the puzzle must not be overlooked: the *culture* of higher education. Universities are individual performer cultures, with structures in place to reward individual performance, for both faculty and students alike. Recognition among faculty goes to individuals who perform as scholars or researchers and, to a lesser extent, as teachers. But at most universities, the typical reward system for faculty focuses on teaching and scholarship, with little to no emphasis on developing students beyond the academic classroom. Even when schools acknowledge faculty who think about the non-academic growth of students as human beings, such institutional acknowledgement runs counter to the professional systems that confer status on scholars for their academic work. As the leader development professional from a top-tier business school noted at the start of this chapter, faculty who want to develop students into leaders often have to do it on their own dime, without much institutional support, which sets staff and students up for suboptimal results. Given the lack of rewards or even encouragement in academia for developing students as leaders, why should we be surprised that few faculty members view such work as part of their professional mandate or develop such skills in their professional repertoire?

Making matters worse, the leader development sphere has one of the lowest barriers to entry of any professional or semi-professional activity. There are no articulated professional standards. There are no formal ethical guidelines or credentialing bodies. One can become a self-appointed leadership expert, coach, professional mentor, thought leader, or guru with little to no formal education, training, or experience in this domain. Reinforced by modern social media strategies, some in the executive coaching and leader development space are more like cult leaders than true leader developers, able to project a popular personal brand and inspirational message to large audiences simply by pouring in more marketing dollars. Increasingly, online delivery of leadership content provides scale that was previously unattainable. Most of this activity is cast as leader development, perhaps with a few process metrics (e.g., how many people enrolled, how much did people enjoy the training) but with no actual evidence of any outcomes that really matter.

This lack of meaningful evidence reflects what we see as one of the most important barriers to progress—specifically, people's willingness to measure what actually works to help people grow. Right now, in nearly all colleges and universities nationwide, the measurement of leader development programming does not appear to be anyone's job; we have yet to discover a single instance of a "vice president for leader development" who is specifically designated to oversee efforts to advance students' leadership abilities and to make sure that such efforts are producing real change. Perhaps part of the reason for this deficit is that measuring the results of social interventions is a risky venture. If you go to the trouble of measuring the outcomes of your hard work and find that all your good intentions (and time, and money, and personnel) resulted in little true change, what do you do? In discovering that you've misspent your budget on programs that don't really make a difference, you have effectively guaranteed that your budget will no longer be yours to control. Who is going to be excited about sending more money your way to spend on continuing *not* to change anything? By treating your work as if it were a social science project, rather than a public relations campaign, you have essentially stood in front of a firing squad and armed it with the devices of your own demise, the ammunition being your own data.

Many who eschew the measurement of leadership training initiatives justify their decision by claiming that it's impossible to accurately measure leadership gains. But in reality, organizations and institutions have had the ability to measure change in leader capacity for decades, at least since the development of the assessment center methodology in the mid-1980s.[36] If they want to, universities can use this type of methodology to measure the difference between leader development activities that are successful and those that are not. Continuously and rigorously measuring outcomes is the antithesis of squandering resources on trendy and only superficially beneficial events, which might well be the central reason some people claim that gains from leader development programs are intangible and unmeasurable: because, in reality, so many programs produce little or nothing to be measured. If you're trying to assess an initiative that produces no outcomes, it's no wonder you fail to find any.

Yet, not many educational institutions prioritize the measurement of programs that actually produce outcomes. From our many conversations with self-proclaimed leader developers, budget concerns are probably the single most often cited reason behind this omission, even though those articulating this limitation are among some of the wealthiest educational institutions in the world—schools that can clearly find funds to channel toward their priorities. Consider, for instance, the rise in popularity of state-of-the-art student centers, equipped with specialty gyms, a hundred or more flat-screen televisions, and indoor pools—or on one campus we visited, an actual "lazy river" that wound through campus. How many millions of dollars are spent on such facilities, all while university administrators proclaim that there simply are not funds available to invest in developing students as leaders? A school offering a budgetary rationale for not using a professional leader development strategy is making a choice and declaring its priorities. This choice is often out of alignment with student interests and the institution's own mission statement. (We will have more to say about this excuse and how to overcome it later.)

On the other side of the equation, even with effective measurement capabilities being well established, there seems to be very little consumer awareness of what constitutes effective leader development. Rather, students, parents, the general public, and administrators themselves appear to have passively accepted the false assertion that leader ability is "intangible" or perhaps an inborn quality that cannot be changed, or they believe the myth that a four-year college degree inherently enhances leadership ability. This acceptance has created fertile ground for the growth of an industry filled with junk books, junk practices, junk courses, and underqualified "experts"—an unintentional fleecing of a public that wants leader development but instead receives something less. Even universities that host excellent academic courses in leadership might not be producing more or better leaders—merely people imbued with an academic understanding of leadership theory and research.

This state of affairs harms students, of course, but in a larger sense, it represents a travesty for the next generation of leaders. Without explicit messages and images to the contrary, students are left with little more than Hollywood—or worse, political—stereotypes on which to build their vision of what a great leader looks like. As one Rice student shared in his leader development plan prior to starting leadership coaching, "I tend to think of successful leaders as being more cutthroat, not open to compromise and friendship." Stereotypes of hierarchical, domineering, Machiavellian leaders prevail as the only way to be a successful leader and turn many young people away from aspiring to leadership roles at all. Ironically, this sort of self-selection process can result in a self-fulfilling prophecy. Those who could bring something else to the table—such as emotional intelligence, respect for others, empathy, and an ability to listen—decide that the table isn't really for them at all, and those who resonate with the stereotype pull up and claim their seat.

This makes accurately assessing leader development programs all the more critical. To avoid investing resources in initiatives that don't really work, the Doerr Institute has created a rigorous evaluation process to measure every program's effectiveness by employing multiple methods to collect a combination of behavioral, observational, and psychological data in ways that fit the purpose and context of each initiative. Having a dedicated measurement team that isn't invested in any particular program (and, thus, can evaluate each program's effects in relatively unbiased ways) is a unique feature of the Doerr Institute's structure. Because of this separation between evaluation and implementation, no one working with students gets to preside over the evaluation their own work. As William Faulkner famously said, "In writing, you must kill all your darlings."[37] Whether it's words, ideas, or training initiatives, that concept can be very difficult for people to embrace. When someone designs a complex, time-intensive intervention to help students grow as leaders, that intervention becomes their "darling," and once it does, it's hard for them to let it go. An independent measurement team makes it as easy as possible to eliminate programs that don't produce the changes we want to see in students by remembering that our ultimate goal is to help students grow as leaders. Armed with clear and compelling data about what's working and what's not, the leader development team at the Institute can make evidence-based decisions about how to develop students as leaders.

Universities possess the means to change the world, one student at a time, by helping students develop a vision, an identity, and a skillset for leading well. With their student bodies composed of a highly filtered, self-selected population (college students, who comprise only about 30 percent of the adult American populace but 94 percent of future leaders in industry, government, the arts, and education[38]), universities shape the future in profound ways. We suggest that most universities are unknowingly missing their transformative potential and losing an opportunity to help nurture the leaders we so desperately need in the world, all the while claiming to be "developing the leaders of tomorrow." If a fact-checker was examining higher education's claims, many schools would earn a "partly true," and some would earn a "mostly false" (or even a "pinocchio"). It's high time that this state of affairs changes.

An Example Framework for Leader Development Programming

Our fundamental argument is that universities have failed to build an effective leader development architecture into their structure. It may be useful to articulate the six deliberate steps that we used at Rice to build the Doerr Institute. To be sure, we don't claim to have THE answer for the creation of a university leader development strategy—there are many good ways to get the job done. That said, we offer below a brief history of how the Doerr Institute developed, and we provide a description of the current programs that emerged from our efforts. We built our institute using the following steps:

1. **Listening.** At the recommendation of Rice University President David Leebron, we sought to listen to key stakeholders in order to understand Rice's culture before formulating a plan. The first author, along with his executive assistant, executed 185 one-hour interviews across the spectrum of stakeholders: faculty, students, deans, vice presidents, the board of trustees, parents, alumni, and community leaders. The interviews gave us a feel for Rice's unique values and norms and helped us identify key components of a successful leader development program at a top research university. It also acculturated key stakeholders to the idea that we were serious about leader development.

2. **"Proof of Principle."** Most start-ups seek early wins. We knew that high-quality coaching tended to produce measurable results, so we set up a small "proof of principle" effort that engaged three professional coaches from outside the university with 12 top students at Rice for multiple sessions. The coaches were handpicked so that coaching competency could be as-

sured, to best test the assumption that undergraduates could, in fact, benefit from professional coaching. The coaches, Danielle Harlan from Stanford, Jen Grace Baron from Yale, and Melanie Polk, a Rice graduate and the principal at Brighthouse Marketing in Phoenix, AZ, were chosen to develop the students.

3. **The Strategic Plan.** Using the proof of principle as a starting point, the Doerr team briefed the university president and the principal donors, Ann and John Doerr, on a way ahead that included professional coaching for students, additional development events, and a measurement protocol that would ensure success. It was approved, and this plan set the stage for a full pilot for program initiatives.

4. **The Pilot Program.** The Doerr Institute recruited 18 professional leadership coaches from the Houston business community on personal service agreements, all certified by the International Coaching Federation (ICF), and created a one-semester coaching experience for 266 undergraduate volunteers. Outcomes were measured by an external measurement consulting firm and pointed to a high potential for one-on-one leader development to impact the ability of individual Rice students to lead. The recruitment of the coaching professionals was embarrassingly simple; the first author went to the ICF Christmas party, made on-the-spot assessments of coaches, and engaged 20. An internet search eliminated two coaches based on some problematic aspects of their online footprint, and the remaining 18 coaches were hired. Outcome measures were similar to the proof of principle—significant gains in student capacity to lead (more on this in a later chapter).

5. **Moving Beyond Coaching.** While we found professional coaching (not mentoring, not advising) to be useful in leader development, we did a similar proof-of-principle and pilot validation of multi-session workshops—a two-hour workshop on a specific skill, followed by two weeks of independent application, followed by another two-hour workshop—and also determined them to be effective and useful. Single session workshops did not produce measurable results. Finally, we validated a group coaching format in which groups of students were professionally coached on a common topic.

6. **Locking in Gains.** Multiple decisions were made to lock in gains. A full-time staff of nine was hired to handle budget

administration, coach management, new program design, and digital communications and marketing. We created an ICF-approved coach certification course, which was originally considered a way to produce our own cadre of coaches. As it turned out, sufficient qualified coaches were already available in Houston, but we continued to certify coaches and used the profits from the course to create a free certification for two sections of 24 students each annually—producing the first undergraduates who were fully qualified as ICF coaches. With our gains locked in, we were able to focus on refinement of all leader development opportunities delivered to students.

The Doerr Institute began with two people listening and currently has 10 full-time employees working with more than 100 additional vendor coaches, facilitators, trainers, student workers (paid and volunteer), and others. The current state of programming includes:

1. One-on-one professional leadership coaching for a semester (typically four to five sessions) in what we call our Activation program;
2. Multi-session workshops on specific competencies, taught in two hours, followed by a two-week break and then two more hours in what we call our Catalyst program;
3. Group coaching for students who are interested in a common topic in what we call our Synthesis program;
4. Excursions into the Houston community to meet with top-tier leaders in business, government, the arts, and the social sector, with a follow-on workshop led by a professional coach and a professional facilitator;
5. A student affiliate advisory group that provides advice and support to peers and gives the affiliates unique training and development opportunities in return;
6. Monetary awards for faculty leadership research proposals and proposals for teaching innovations that develop leaders in the classroom;
7. A leadership stipend, offered to students who wish to occupy a leadership role while at Rice but whose financial circumstances require income from an outside job (competitive, to a limited number of students in conjunction with the Office of Financial Aid);
8. A professional organization development consultancy that

works at the request of student leaders to improve the leadership and management of student organizations;

9. An International Coaching Federation certification course
(called CoachRICE: Students) for students who wish to pursue formal certification as a leadership coach or to develop
coaching skills as a leader;

10. A training process for orientation week coordinators to assist
those students in completing their leadership role in accultur-
ating new students;

11. An International Coaching Federation certification course
(called CoachRICE: Professional) facing outward to the
Houston business community and beyond, including a dedicated course that is internal to a large cancer treatment and
research center that provides coach training of staff in support
of more than 20,000 employees.

Of these programs, only the coaching course offered to the business
community is fee-based; the remaining programs and services are free of
charge to students. All programs are offered to all graduate and undergraduate students from all seven schools at Rice (architecture, business,
engineering, humanities, music, natural sciences, social sciences). No students are required to take any program, and in keeping with research on
internal versus external motivation, no program is externally incentivized
by course credit. There are also a number of activities that we examined
or piloted ourselves but do NOT offer, based on excessive expense, a poor
track record of developmental gains, or both. Those activities include:

1. Leadership speakers or speaker series *#
2. Dinner discussions with faculty #
3. Academic leadership courses *#
4. Week-long outdoor activities with facilitators *
5. Weekend retreats *#
6. Full-time internal coaching staff (vs. vendors) *
7. Single session workshops #
8. Mentor programs or programming with non-certified coaches #

* *Too expensive*

Minimal or no outcome effects on measured capacity to lead

Some of these activities are quite popular as leadership offerings on campuses, including at Rice. To be clear, we don't condemn these activities for schools that find ways to make them affordable to run and effective at producing measurable increases in students' capacity to lead. But from our rigorous measurement perspective, and given the need for us to maintain a lean business model to offer training to all students, these activities simply did not work for us.

In the chapters that follow, we will describe the programs that do work for us in more detail, starting with a deeper explanation of what coaching is. Throughout this book, we will tell student stories of growth and change (but note that all student names have been changed to protect their identities). We will also describe some of the evidence we have accumulated to demonstrate outcomes associated with effective programs as examples, and we will elaborate on our core operating principles that we think could be adopted at any institution that is interested in doing a better job developing students as leaders.

FOR REFLECTION: A Reality Check on Your Approach to Leader Development

Are you really taking leader development seriously at your institution, or is leader development just a public relations claim? To decide, ask yourself the following challenge questions:

1. The core functions of an institution always have someone specifically in charge of them (e.g., a vice president, a dean). Is there one person at your institution who oversees the development of students as leaders? If so, what is this person's place in the institutional hierarchy?

2. How would a rival institution characterize the core elements of your leader development work? Would they be on solid ground to describe most of what passes as leader development at your institution as being "leader-tainment" rather than true development of the ability to lead well?

3. If an intervention matters to us, we usually look for evidence that the intervention is working. Have you ever asked anyone at your institution for empirical evidence that the leader

development work that's happening is doing good? Can you (as well as prospective employers) distinguish the top leading graduates from the mediocre ones? If not, why not?

Chapter 2

USING PROFESSIONALS TO ACHIEVE PROFESSIONAL RESULTS:

Coaching as a Tool for Leader Development

Like most universities, Rice's mission statement explicitly referenced the aspiration to develop leaders, but the university was falling short when it came to acting on this part of the mission. As noted in the Introduction, when John Doerr informally met a few dozen Rice seniors before delivering his 2007 commencement address, his observations were not flattering. It wasn't because the students weren't smart, he said. Rather, they lacked the presence and self-confidence that he expected to find in a group of young leaders.

This encounter led to the launch of the Doerr Institute for New Leaders in 2015, which established one-on-one, professional coaching as one of its most critical tools. John Doerr is a big believer in professional coaching to develop leaders. In *Measure What Matters*, he credits the late Bill Campbell as the "master coach" who helped develop more great leaders than probably anyone else in Silicon Valley.[39] Kleiner, Perkins, Caufield, and Byers (the venture capital firm chaired by Doerr) called upon Campbell time after time to coach the leaders in whom Doerr was investing. Eric Schmidt, former CEO of Google, was initially offended when Doerr suggested that he needed to be coached. A year after following Doerr's suggestion, he had become a believer: "Bill Campbell has been very helpful in coaching all of us. In hindsight, his role was needed from the beginning," said Schmidt.[40]

But some readers might be asking, "How does a professional leadership coach actually increase a person's capacity to lead?"

Outside of the business world, few people know much about professional leadership coaching (sometimes called "executive coaching"), much less have any personal experience working with a leadership coach. Furthermore, the industry is teeming with specialists who call themselves coaches, though many lack any formal training or credentials.* As a result, our suggestion that schools consider using professional coaching to help students develop might be met with some skepticism, and it's also likely to create some confusion among people at academic institutions. At the end of Chapter 1, we described in broad terms how we use coaching across several of our core programs for developing students as leaders. In this chapter, we will describe in more detail what we mean when we use the word "coaching," and we will provide readers with some detailed guidance on how to set up and manage a coaching system at their own institution. In the rest of the book, we will reference our own coaching program and the evidence we have gathered for its effectiveness as a tool for developing students as leaders.

The Value of Coaching for Leaders and Organizations

Research from Globoforce, a workplace performance and employee engagement company, found that "as organizations evaluate their performance management processes, coaching is seen as very important," with close to three quarters of HR professionals indicating that formal or informal coaching of employees is very important or somewhat important at their organization.[41] Yet the same survey showed nearly all managers surveyed—93 percent—said that they still needed training on how to effectively coach their employees. This disconnect between leaders' espoused values and their admitted lack of competency is not surprising given that so few universities offer leadership training and coaching to their students. How can we expect managers to know how to coach people when they've never been taught coaching skills themselves? With this in view, the Doerr Institute prioritizes not only coaching students to develop their own leadership skills but also training students to coach and develop their peers through CoachRICE, a program that we describe later in this chapter.

Coaching is both a valuable leadership competency and an increasingly expected one throughout corporate America. As reported recently in *Forbes*, in the business world, working with a leadership coach is predicted

---

* The ICF, which we've mentioned already, is one of the largest credentialing organizations for professional coaches in the world, alongside the International Coaching Community, or ICC.

to become the norm for executives, and some even predict that it might overtake consulting over the next decade.[42] The global leadership coaching industry was estimated at approximately $2 billion in 2017, which reflects a noticeable percentage of the total dollars spent on developing leaders worldwide, with a commensurate "dramatic increase in coaches, professional coaching organizations, and coaching-related research."[43] According to the ICF, there are currently more than 53,000 professional coaches worldwide, with the highest number of coaches in Western Europe and North America.[44] As of June 2020, there were more than 30,000 practicing coaches holding a professional credential from the ICF, with designations of Associate, Professional, or Master Coach.[45] These coaches have focuses that include life coaching, business coaching, executive coaching, career coaching, leadership coaching, and internal coaching.[46]

The Doerr Institute's use of professional coaching as part of its core approach to leader development reflects both the growth of the profession across diverse industry sectors and a documented need for the benefits that coaching provides. Although coaching occurs primarily in the senior executive space,[47] that is not the ideal time in one's career path to develop as a leader. Older leaders typically receive the lion's share of coaching investments because companies are looking for ways to maximize the impact of their training and development budgets. Why invest in an early-career, lower-level manager who is likely to leave for another company when you could invest in leaders who are already working in upper management and whose impact on the company, for better or worse, is much greater than the impact of a low-level manager? It might be no coincidence, too, that top executives are the ones responsible for allocating training expenses and resources.

In contrast to this executive-oriented approach in industry, the Doerr Institute sees a transformational opportunity for universities that are willing to intervene early in a student's career and expand the leadership pipeline exponentially. In support of this perspective, we conducted an anonymous survey of 18 professional leadership coaches within our own program. These coaches had experience coaching college students as well as executives. We asked these coaches a series of questions about whether they thought college students or executives seemed more open and able to change through coaching. The table below shows the results of this (admittedly small) survey. Coaches often believed that neither group was more changeable than the other, but when they thought one group was more changeable, it was almost always college students.

Table 1. Judgments by professional coaches as to whether students or executives were more open to change through coaching

	Students	Neither	Executives
1. More open to change	50.0%	44.4%	5.6%
2. More open to new ways of thinking	50.0%	50.0%	0.0%
3. More likely to grow in self-awareness	33.3%	55.6%	11.1%
4. More likely to change their behaviors	44.4%	55.6%	0.0%

Coaching as a Unique Tool for Change

Because of the unregulated nature of the coaching industry, we often use the term "professional coaching" in this book to differentiate the work of trained coach practitioners from the informal practices of other leader developers. Additionally, we separate professional leadership coaching from other developmental relationships, such as mentoring or counseling. Many professionals claim to provide "coaching" to their clients, but they are not "partnering with clients in a thought-provoking and creative process that inspires them to maximize their personal and professional potential," which is the definition of professional coaching offered by the ICF.[48] Although there are several other reasonable definitions of professional coaching that have been used in the academic literature,[49] we find that the ICF's definition does a good job of capturing the essence of what we mean when we use the term, and it allows us to differentiate between professional coaching and other forms of social interventions (e.g., mentoring, consulting). We should acknowledge, as well, that the ICF approach to coaching is not the only school of thought regarding how coaching should be practiced. We have found, though, that this approach works very well in a university context, and it might be particularly suited to helping students develop as leaders, as opposed to more senior managers or executives further along in their careers. The description of coaching that we offer below derives from this ICF perspective on the nature of professional coaching.

Professional coaching is not therapy, although coaching and therapy use some similar skill sets and tools. A therapist provides interventions to clients to help them with mental health needs. Coaches do not work in the space of psychological disorders but within the realm of more commonplace needs and goals. Neither is professional coaching the same as mentoring. As we have already noted, mentors provide advice, usually life or career-related, based upon their experience and relative seniority. Mentors are most often untrained and uncredentialed, and the outcomes of mentoring are rarely assessed. Likewise, professional coaching is not teaching or consulting. The coach does not *tell* the client what to do or think. (To reiterate, this characterization of the practice of coaching reflects the ICF model, not every school of thought about coaching). The coach does not *direct* the client to a particular goal or strategy or insist that the client adopt a particular solution. The nature of the coaching relationship, unlike in teaching or consulting, is not characterized by one person handing down knowledge, wisdom, or solutions from a position of authority or power. Rather, the coach adopts a posture characterized by the phrase "leading from behind." This posture is one that we have found to be especially powerful in our own work helping students develop their leadership abilities.

The approach that a leadership coach takes might best be described by the phrase "humble inquiry."[50] A coach uncovers beliefs and motivations by asking questions. A coach listens, both to what is said and what is not said. A coach makes neutral observations and provides feedback, sometimes in the form of formal assessment results, but the coach does not *direct*. The client is in charge and drives the agenda in a coaching engagement. The client's priorities, goals, and aspirations determine the direction that a coaching engagement will take. A coach might, on occasion, challenge a client's interpretation of an event or behavior or offer an alternate viewpoint, but even when challenging, the coach remains unattached to his or her opinion. In adopting this "leading from behind" posture, the coach capitalizes on the power of the client's intrinsic motivation to pursue his or her own goals and aspirations, which is critical if real change is to occur. By building a relationship of trust and psychological safety, the coach creates the space for a client to explore, reflect, and assess his or her behavior, drivers, and ambitions.

Change is difficult. It needs to be fueled by powerful and self-reinforcing drivers. Typically in coaching, those drivers come from the client's own vision of an ideal self or positive future. A variety of academic studies have examined whether professional coaching is effective as an intervention strategy, most often in the realm of business, and the results of these studies have generally been quite positive.[51] We should underscore, however, that asking whether "coaching works" is somewhat like asking whether "training works." There are many types of training, and there are many types of trainers and training models. Likewise, any assessment of the efficacy of coaching must take into consideration the qualifications of the coaches involved, the type of coaching used, the length of the coaching process, whether coaching is mandatory or voluntary, the nature of the organization within which the coaching is occurring, and the types of outcomes used to evaluate the engagement, among many other considerations.

Despite such complexities, there are several meaningful conclusions that can be derived from the academic study of professional leadership coaching to date. In short, coaching can be a very effective tool to develop leaders. At present, the number of randomized controlled trials examining the efficacy of coaching is quite modest, but a recent meta-analysis of these studies concluded that professional coaching causes positive changes across a variety of outcomes, ranging from hope to self-regulation to well-being.[52] In this meta-analysis, the authors found a small trend toward greater efficacy of coaching for younger people than for older people, which echoes a finding from a larger meta-analysis on leadership training more broadly (including, but not limited to, professional coaching).[53] We should note in this regard that "younger people" in the coaching meta-analysis referred to those under the age of 30, with the parallel in the leadership training meta-analysis being lower-level leaders (versus higher-level leaders).

Student Experiences with Leadership Coaching

Personal insights and paradigm shifts are common among students who have participated in the Doerr Institute's coaching program. Julie, for instance, had worked in the energy field in China prior to enrolling at Rice to attain her master's degree in global affairs and to make connections in Houston's energy industry. She learned about the Institute through our outreach to international students. Like many incoming students, Julie was initially unfamiliar with the coaching process, but she welcomed the idea of developing her leadership skills, particularly because she viewed herself as lacking in confidence.

When she began one-on-one coaching, Julie expected her coach to provide her with advice and suggestions. Instead, to her surprise, her coach began asking questions that helped her reach her own conclusions about what she needed to do. Julie shared that, as part of her cultural upbringing, she was used to following instructions from parents, teachers, and bosses, so challenging herself to make her own decisions was a new—and even frightening—experience for her. But as she began to understand the self-directed nature of the coaching process, she set an objective to learn to express her ideas and views more freely.

Slowly and painstakingly, Julie overcame her tendency to hold back and started to take more risks by airing her thoughts in both social and academic contexts. In the classroom, a venue in which she had previously been fearful even to raise her hand, she started speaking up and excitedly discovered that her classmates and professors were often fascinated by what she had to say. She found that her "difference" in being Chinese was not a detriment at all but rather an asset, as people were eager to hear her international perspective.

Ultimately, as a result of her coaching conversations, Julie found the courage to revisit an early career goal—working in journalism—which she had previously abandoned after listening to others' opinions that joining the energy sector was more practical and realistic. She had always wanted to be a journalist, and when the opportunity arose for a summer journalism internship at a news agency in China, she took it. Julie described her newfound confidence as "feeling the fire from the bottom of my heart," which empowered her to overcome cultural expectations and pursue her independent goals.

In Chapter 5, we will describe some of the quantitative evidence we've accumulated for the impact of coaching. But sometimes more qualitative, narrative feedback about a program or intervention can be helpful in addition to charts, graphs, and statistical reports. With this in mind, we always ask students to tell us in their own words what they found useful about the coaching experience (as well as how we could improve it). Here is a small sample of the kind of survey-based feedback that students give us about the value of professional coaching:

- "My coach was able to synthesize observations about my behavior in a way that I was not able to see before to help me create new goals for my development."
- "My coach asked really insightful and helpful questions that helped me have a clearer vision of what kind of leader I want to be."

- "This program taught me a lot about how to work with people and how to work *with* my emotions instead of working *against* them."
- "I came away with a better understanding of my limitations as a leader and clear action steps of how I could change."
- "Just forcing myself to admit certain things aloud to a coach and verbalize what I wanted to work on made me more dedicated to working on these characteristics than I have been in the past."
- "I have never gotten to simultaneously see myself as critically and compassionately as I did through my coach's coaching. I am so grateful for the patient dedication of my coach to helping me improve and the space offered me for honest reflection. I only wish I had joined the Doerr Institute program sooner."

In addition to providing students with valuable self-insights, professional coaching promotes inclusiveness on campus by ensuring that all students at Rice have the opportunity (if they take it) to receive individually tailored support and guidance to address their unique needs and challenges while also empowering those with diverse backgrounds to take on leadership roles.

Jerome experienced this firsthand and shared that he found his participation in the Doerr Institute's leadership training and coaching empowered him to make a difference by co-creating a student organization at Rice. Jerome explained that because of the university's emphasis on inclusion, students of color sometimes find themselves "separated within campus, because a part of diversity and inclusion is that you want to be diverse in whom you experience and interact with." This is particularly true in the residence halls, which intentionally include a wide mix of people hailing from different backgrounds and experiences. While Jerome believes there are benefits to such an approach, he also feels it can make it more challenging to meet others with shared identities. To bridge this gap, he took on a leadership role to help create that sense of community by co-founding the Black Male Leadership Initiative. He also became involved with the Young Owls Leadership Program, which helps to train underrepresented high school students in leadership skills.

Although he had been serving in leadership roles before participating in the Doerr Institute, Jerome credits the combined experience of being coached and learning to coach others with helping him understand what it really means to be a leader: "I didn't know what leadership development really looked like before. We called ourselves the Black Male Leadership Initiative, and we really wanted to *be* the Black Male Leadership Initiative. So I had to understand what being a leader was and to pass down the reins to the next leader."

Selecting, Training, and Evaluating Professional Coaches

In 2004, *Harvard Business Review* published an article by Stratford Sherman and Alyssa Freas who described "the untamed terrain of executive coaching" and compared it to the Wild West for being "chaotic, largely unexplored, and fraught with risk, yet immensely promising."[54] Because there are few barriers to entry in the field, people with little to no experience or formal training can hang out a shingle and declare themselves an expert at coaching employees and executives. "At best, the coaching certifications offered by various self-appointed bodies are difficult to assess, while methods of measuring return on investment are questionable," wrote Sherman and Freas.[55]

While it's still true that anyone can claim to be an executive coach, the rise of advanced coaching certifications has helped separate the professionals from the amateurs. For this reason, the Doerr Institute only uses coaches who have certifications from the ICF. Each coach is carefully screened, trained, and measured—not just once but for every single coaching engagement—to ensure that students benefit from the highest level of ethics, expertise, and outcomes.

In her role managing all of the coaching-related programs at the Doerr Institute, Ruth Reitmeier, an ICF-certified coach, emphasizes that for coaching to be effective, it must be predicated on proper selection, training, and management of coaches. Reitmeier provides oversight for over 2,000 individual coaching sessions every year, including creating structure and maintaining standards while allowing independent coaches to create individualized engagements. Ensuring high-quality coaching that produces measureable outcomes is the ultimate goal. Reitmeier explains:

> There's a lot of coaching out there that is not skillful. It's not culturally sensitive, and I don't think it promotes the psychological safety for people to change. I think that skilled, trained coaches are like

surgeons. They know how to go in and do no harm. They have the empathy to support people as they take risks and try new things. They have the sensitivity to help a client overcome barriers and to face and acknowledge failures. As a coach, if you have the patience to support the client over the course of that engagement, then you're a champion for change in their life. You see something in them, you believe in them, and it helps them believe in themselves.

To this end, the Doerr Institute puts a great deal of thought into how it selects and professionally develops its coaches. Just because a coach has a professional certification from ICF or another accrediting body doesn't mean that he or she will be a good fit for working with college students in a highly competitive environment. Hence, once the coaching process is underway, outcomes are measured from the perspective of the students and from the perspective of each coach. Growth and development are measured with valid psychological instruments. Coaches who don't produce results (20 percent in the first cohort of coaches, now less than 5 percent) are not asked back.

The work of leadership coaches begins with seeing the potential within each student—to understand both who they are and who they want to become and to partner with them in their development so that they can increase their capacity to lead. Coaches and student clients forge a working alliance built on trust and transparency. Students and coaches work together to honestly assess current leadership capacity: what's working, what's not working, what skills or knowledge gaps exist. Next they co-create a vision for where the student wants to go or who he or she wants to become. The most critical piece is defining concrete goals and determining what action steps need to be taken to achieve those goals.

We recently explored what makes for a truly successful coaching engagement. How can we know what factors lead to successful and measurable outcomes? To address this question, we conducted an internal study of our own coaching program in a sample of 115 students who completed three to five sessions of professional coaching over the course of a semester. In this study, we compared three factors that might contribute to students' goal progress: specifically, students' engagement levels (as rated by their coaches), coaches' levels of supportiveness (as rated by their student clients), and the extent to which students and coaches co-created effective goal pursuit plans (also as rated by students). Coaches' evaluations of students' engagement levels were measured with a 7-item scale, including items such as "This student typically showed up prepared for the session" and "This student was typically highly engaged throughout the session." Students' ratings of their coaches' levels of supportiveness were measured with an 8-item scale that included items such as "My coach supported me in attaining my goals" and "My coach demonstrated an openness to understand my personal challenge(s) as a leader." Finally, the extent to which coaches and students co-created effective goal pursuit plans was measured with a 3-item scale, including items such as "With my coach, I set specific goals" and "I created specific action steps related to my goals with my coach."

We used all three of the factors to predict students' own ratings of the extent to which they made meaningful progress toward one or more of their leadership goals over the course of the semester. These student ratings of goal progress were themselves significantly predicted by coaches' observations of goal-related progress, which validated students' goal progress ratings as an outcome variable.[*] All three factors contributed independently to the prediction of students' leadership-related goal progress during the semester. (In other words, each factor was a statistically significant predictor in the model.) Together, these three factors accounted for over half the variation in students' goal progress levels. However, these factors were not equally important contributors to students' goal progress. The figure below graphically illustrates the relative importance of the three predictor variables from a regression model that also included several statistical control variables (specifically, the number of coaching sessions, whether students were undergraduates or graduate students, students' gender, and whether students were international or domestic). As this figure shows, the most important predictor of student progress was the co-creation of effective goal pursuit plans, followed by coach supportiveness, and then student engagement.

---

[*] Specifically, coaches' observations of student goal progress were significantly correlated with students' own ratings of their goal progress, $r = .33, p < .001$.

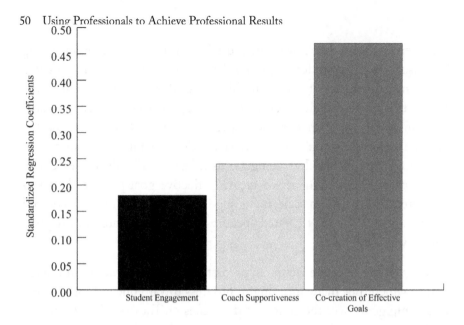

Figure 3. The relative importance of three predictors of student goal progress

Individualized Coaching within a Structured Coaching Framework

We work with many different types of emerging student leaders at Rice. For example, a coach might be paired with an ambivalent student who needs to address underlying assumptions about what a leader is and what leadership looks like and who might have a distorted or limiting view of what leaders are "supposed" to do. That student would require different development opportunities, tools, and strategies to produce meaningful behavior change than, for example, a student who is currently in a leadership role but feels insecure and riddled with self-doubt, a student who enjoys leading but lacks self-awareness, or an emerging leader who is doing well but wisely senses a growing need for additional skills and training. Consequently, to be effective, our coaches must skillfully weave a sensitivity to the individuality of each student client with the structure that we require within our coaching program—following the general framework that we have outlined for our coaching engagements but tailoring the experience to the needs of each client.

Because every client is unique and has different developmental needs, professional coaching work is necessarily challenging and requires balancing art and science, wisdom and skill. Coaches are encouraged to work closely with students to gain in-depth knowledge about their needs and tailor recommendations for next steps in their leadership development. To this end, coaches agree to uphold the following Doerr Institute Coaching Best Practices:

1. Treat the student as your partner.
2. Listen more than you talk—which may be challenging with students with low self-expression skills or an introverted personality.
3. Maintain professional boundaries—avoid nurturing, parenting, counseling.
4. Keep a curious mind—stay out of judgment.
5. Be sensitive to cultural differences.
6. Keep coaching client-centered—go where the client goes.
7. Ask clarifying questions—search for underlying meaning if intuition tells you there might be more.
8. Provide observations.
9. Ensure confidentiality.
10. Be flexible and adaptable—what worked before might not work here.

To inform ongoing coach training and ensure that our students are benefitting from the most effective coaching possible, measurement is vital. *Forbes* highlighted in 2018 that "[w]hat will set successful executive coaches apart from others in the coming years is their ability to demonstrate measurable results."[56] With this in mind, students complete short, online surveys after every coaching session to help document their experience. These surveys, which can be taken from a smart phone or computer, are themselves tailored to the Institute's coaching framework. Survey questions for the first two sessions focus on chemistry between the coach and student and on the insights gained (or not) through feedback from a measure of emotional intelligence that the student completes prior to the first coaching session. (We will talk in more depth about the concept of emotional intelligence in the next chapter.) Starting after the third session, survey questions focus on goal setting, action planning, and progress. These surveys are created to trigger email alerts to Doerr Institute staff whenever a student gives a low rating to his or her coach on key survey questions. With this structured approach, we can identify instances of poor fit between the coach and client from the very beginning of the process and intervene as appropriate. We have also been able to determine that a student's level of goal-related progress at the end of the semester can be predicted by the student's feedback as early as the first session.

Can Students Learn Coaching Skills? The CoachRICE Initiative

"There's no question that organizations need to get better at 'coaching the coaches' or risk losing their best people....Just because someone is a stellar individual contributor doesn't mean they have the ability to (or that they even want to) inspire a team of people to achieve great work," states Sarah Payne of Globoforce.[57] In the context of the quote above, "coaching the coaches" refers to ensuring people in management positions receive the proper training to effectively lead their team, a process that rarely happens in a timely manner today. "Coaching the coaches" ahead of time—before students actually begin their careers and assume leadership positions in industry—is what CoachRICE is all about—to supplement the opportunity to be coached with learning skills for coaching others.

In their book, *Trillion Dollar Coach*, Eric Schmidt, Jonathan Rosenberg, and Alan Eagle, who served as leaders at Google for over a decade, assert that "being a good coach is essential to being a good manager and leader. Coaching is no longer a specialty. You cannot be a good manager without being a good coach."[58] Indeed, Google found in a multiyear, internal study of its own managers that coaching competence was one of 10 skills that distinguished more effective managers from less effective ones.[59] With such findings in view, the Doerr Institute partnered with a world-renowned cancer hospital in the city of Houston to help it develop an ICF-approved coach training program. The purpose of this program was to inculcate professional coaching skills among their senior leaders to create a "coaching culture" at the hospital. As of this writing, more than 75 leaders at that organization have been trained through this program, with more on the way. We suspect it's no coincidence that the hospital recently won a national award for leader development by the National Center for Healthcare Leadership.

If coaching skills are the new requirement for leadership in the 21st century, then universities need to consider how they are preparing students to meet these expectations. CoachRICE, the Doerr Institute's coach training program, is the only program of its kind in higher education. It is an intensive, year-long training program for students who have benefited from coaching and now seek to develop this skill set for themselves. It's the only program at the Doerr Institute that has a prerequisite, and for good reason: we feel it is vital for students to understand coaching from the perspective of being coached before they commit to becoming coaches themselves. The program is only open to students who have successfully completed a full semester (typically five sessions) of one-on-one coaching.

The rigorous, 60-hour CoachRICE program is accredited by ICF and uses a blend of modalities and methods to equip students to become more collaborative, creative, and compassionate leaders by increasing their self-awareness and growing their listening and questioning skills. The program's learning goals include identifying the core competencies for effectiveness as a leadership coach; distinguishing how coaching differs from consulting, mentoring, and therapy; and increasing participants' ability to reflect, notice, respond to feedback, and self-correct.

Students see CoachRICE as a way to enhance their personal leadership skills and have noted specific behavioral changes they've incorporated into their own leadership. As one CoachRICE student explained:

> I wanted to develop my leadership skills beyond my coaching sessions and continue the momentum for my personal growth as a leader. This training has helped me become a better listener, a more reflective individual, and a more well-rounded human being. This training…gave me more confidence as a leader and taught me to be more self-aware of my presence and identity as a leader.

Another student from the same cohort reported that CoachRICE training led her to the realization that being a leader is about empowering others—a new understanding that ultimately changed the behaviors and competencies that this student drew on as a leader:

> At its core, [leadership] is a form of service to and for others, and I absolutely love that. I used to think leadership was kind of "buzzword-y" and self-serving, but this training has made me realize that I was very wrong. Now, I will be moving forward in life trying to maintain this focus on others and nudging them toward finding their own solutions and reaching their own goals in their own way.

To determine the extent to which students have attained the level of proficiency that CoachRICE aims for, professional leadership coaches serve as observers throughout the program. As students practice their coaching and communication skills on each other, these professional observers provide feedback about what they are doing well and where they need more practice. At the end of the course, these professional coaches also rate how ready each student is to submit a recording of their coaching skills to the ICF in pursuit of their coaching credential (on a scale ranging from 1 [not at all ready] to 7 [completely ready]). Similar observers have used the same readiness rating system in two distinct cohorts of adults who have independently completed CoachRICE programs—one in a community-facing training program at Rice and the other in the local hospital that we mentioned earlier. The percentages across these three cohorts of students and professionals that were judged as being ready to pursue ICF credentials (meaning the participants scored a 5 or better on the 7-point readiness rating scale) are presented in Table 2. The ratings reveal that Rice students have been judged as being just as ready to pursue their ICF credentials as the adult participants in these other CoachRICE training programs, which shows that students can, indeed, learn to coach others.

Table 2. Student readiness ratings provided by professional coach observers across three cohorts of CoachRICE

	N	% Rated as Ready to Pursue ICF Credentials
Student Cohort	21	84%
Professional Cohort	24	71%
Hospital Cohort	24	88%

After discussions with multiple institutions of higher education about the value of professional coaching for students, we have noticed a recurring theme: most universities said that the main reason they don't use coaching as part of their leader development training is a lack of funding. This financial excuse, which we will argue against in Chapter 6, is one that we have even heard from Ivy League schools—institutions with multi-billion-dollar endowments that clearly have sufficient resources for their true priorities.

As a university program on the front lines of using professional coaching as a method for leader development, the Doerr Institute has developed a viable business model that should counter protests about financial barriers. We've discovered that individualized coaching, delivered by part-time vendor coaches, is much less expensive than many people expect—about half the cost of a semester-long classroom course. But the *impact* of coaching, described throughout this book (and in detail in Chapter 5), is equally important to the financial case for using professional coaching. Instead of creating expensive, contrived "leadership events" that are meant primarily to entertain rather than to develop students' identities or skills, professional coaching is delivered in the context of each student's current activities, roles, and passions, which ensures relevance and enhances impact for long-term growth. Offering formal coach training to students as well gives them valuable leadership skills they can use to develop others, whether or not they decide to become certified leadership coaches down the road.

Conclusion

In 2019, John and Ann Doerr returned to Rice to assess the impact of the institute that bore their name, four years after its founding. During a fireside chat in the business school library, they met with a group of students who had worked with the Doerr Institute. These students were poised, articulate, and eager to share stories of their personal growth as leaders. They jockeyed to get seats up close so that they could hear and made small talk with Ann as John signed copies of his recent book. The informal gathering included students who had been involved with the Institute in one-on-one coaching, CoachRICE, and other leader competency trainings. The senior venture capitalist described what he saw in these students as nothing short of "spectacular." Said Doerr regarding the Institute:

> It's more than an experiment. I think it's a wise bet. I think we'll see three, four, five years from now in controlled, measured studies that the Rice undergrads and grads who chose to be part of these various leadership activities are going to be making a bigger difference in the world.

We will have a great deal more to say throughout this book about the evidence we have gathered for short-term changes in students as a result of coaching and other training that the Doerr Institute provides. Although our investigations are ongoing and it's too early to draw any definitive conclusions about the long-term impact of our work with students, the final chapter of this book will describe some preliminary findings with alums that have been very encouraging. Given previous studies that have examined evidence for the power of coaching in the business world, in addition to the evidence we will discuss later regarding the impact of coaching as a leader development tool for students, we are optimistic that coaching is, indeed, a powerful tool for change, and we believe that institutions of higher education that use this tool will be convinced of its value as well. In the next two chapters, we continue this discussion of foundational tools and concepts that colleges and universities should consider carefully as they design and evaluate their own leader development programs, starting with the concepts of leader identity and emotional intelligence.

FOR REFLECTION: Are You Effectively Coaching Your Coaches?

There's more to managing a world-class, professional leadership program for students than pairing students up with professional coaches. Even when you hire only ICF-certified coaches, it's still critical to ensure that you provide them with the knowledge and resources they need to understand the unique needs of your students, your leader development program, and your university. Ask yourself the challenge questions below:

1. Do you provide coaches with clear, best practices that reflect the unique priorities and values of your program and school?
2. Do you regularly communicate the mission and vision of your program so that coaches are functioning as a cohesive unit and not independent practitioners?
3. Do you have a person responsible for ongoing training and supervision of your coaches?
4. Do you evaluate the performance of your coaches in order to intervene in a timely fashion when a student-coach pairing is not working and to ultimately judge whether each coach is effectively developing leaders?
5. Have you considered helping students develop their own coaching skills as part of their leadership repertoire?

Chapter 3

BUILDING A STRONG FOUNDATION:

The Development of Leader Identity and Emotional Intelligence

Ronaldo was heavily involved in leadership roles during high school. In addition to serving as concert master in his school's orchestra and mentoring middle schoolers through his church, he was also captain of his championship football team, on which he played safety, a position that is, effectively, the "quarterback of the defense." As team captain, he developed the quality of perseverance, especially during the most intense training period before the season started (the infamous "two-a-days," which were made all the more brutal by the scorching Texas sun). This quality was not merely the product of having to manage his own pain and desire to quit during those soul-crushing workouts but the result of doing so while also focusing on the younger members of the team, who he knew were on the verge of quitting at any moment.

This ability to focus on his younger teammates while managing his own suffering would serve him well when he joined the United States Naval Academy (USNA). Perhaps just as important as his experience of being captain of the football team, the hours he had spent mentoring middle schoolers from church would prove invaluable as well. Few sane adults would be willing to relive their middle school years, fraught as they are with social conflict, physical changes, identity questions, and existential crises. The emotional burdens that this cocktail of psychological suffering can produce cause some fragile teens to begin contemplating suicide as a form of escape, as Ronaldo learned first-hand with the middle schoolers he had counseled through these troubled waters. Critically, he learned that being a leader is not about having all the answers all the time for every problem presented to you. An effective leader has the humility to seek the expertise of others to solve problems that the leader can't solve alone. Just so, Ronaldo discovered the importance of being a listening ear and empathetic friend to mentees who were struggling with suicidal thoughts and impulses but quickly letting other, more capable adults take over to make sure that these students received the help they needed from people with the resources and training to help them best. This was a script that would later repeat itself at the Naval Academy.

When the authors of this book spoke with this midshipman during his senior year about his experiences at the USNA, we were reminded of how seriously the United States's military service academies take the development of their students as leaders. Ronaldo described the examples of responsibility that midshipmen like him come to take on over time— learning both how to lead well and how to follow well—and the depth of feedback that he and his peers received regarding their leadership skills. "We are rated on multiple dimensions every semester, first by our company officer, then by upperclassmen, then by our peers, and then by midshipmen below us," he noted. These ratings are supplemented with more open-ended, narrative feedback about both what midshipmen are doing well and ways in which they could stand to improve. Feedback from "above" is always linked to the name of the person providing it, whereas feedback from "below" is always anonymous. Such 360° feedback is a benefit that few college students outside of the military academies will experience, and it is complemented by formal classroom training on leadership, self-reflection exercises, modeling and mentoring, and opportunities to take all of these abstract lessons and put them into practice in real leadership roles.

Ronaldo's own feedback and ratings (which are all shown on his cumulative "scorecard" for every semester at the Naval Academy) describe vividly his developmental journey as a leader. Early on, he learned that he needed to become more direct in giving negative feedback to subordinates. "I was being too soft," he said. "I didn't want to hurt anyone's feelings or seem abusive." This desire is likely what made him the person that peers would often go to for support when the pressures of the Naval Academy felt overwhelming and they were feeling distraught. Rather than being defensive at this "too soft" feedback, Ronaldo took it to heart and realized that direct feedback can be a gift when it is sincere and constructive. Hence, he needn't shy away from telling subordinates what they needed to do when they were failing to pull their weight or fulfill their responsibilities. Younger students needed such honesty in order to self-correct, and he would be failing them profoundly by sugar-coating his feedback or framing it as nothing but a casual suggestion, as he was prone to do.

We offer a closer look at leader development in the service academies, and what all of us can learn from these institutions, in Chapter 7. For now, though, we highlight two elements we believe are critical to effective leader development that the service academies also seem to make a priority. First, these institutions invest in the development of their students' leader identities by giving them increasing levels of leadership responsibilities that help them to see themselves as leaders, develop their confidence, and enhance their willingness to lead. Second, the service academies pay attention to more than just academic feedback for students. As Ronaldo found, they also provide intensive feedback on a regular basis across a wide range of "soft skills" that research shows are essential for effective leaders—skills that rely on what is often referred to as "emotional intelligence." In fact, the type of feedback Ronaldo received about the need to be more direct with subordinates, a counterbalance to his already high levels of kindness, is an important ingredient in the success of interventions designed to boost people's emotional intelligence.[60]

In this chapter, we will talk about these two foundational elements—leader identity and emotional intelligence. While the latter, especially, is a topic that academic scholars love to argue about on statistical and conceptual grounds (e.g., "Should we really call it an 'intelligence'?" and "How much of emotional intelligence is really just an extension of basic personality?"), our treatment of these subjects will be less academic and more practical. The best leaders need more than just book smarts and technical skills to be effective, as anyone who has ever been led can attest. But before people are likely to be given the chance to lead, they must come to identify themselves as leaders. It is with this element that we begin.

The Cognitive Component of Leader Development: Leader Identity

Carlos entered the engineering program at Rice University with a clear dream: to become an entrepreneur. But within his major's curriculum and among his fellow students, he found it difficult to find role models to guide his vision for launching a start-up. "You get the message about what you should be doing, even though deep down you know it isn't what you *want* to be doing," said Carlos. At a crossroads, he began working with a leadership coach through the Doerr Institute. With insights gained through the coaching experience about his leadership strengths and the attributes that could support a nonstandard path for an engineer, he decided it was acceptable to him to be just a *good* engineer if that meant that he could focus his energy and drive on becoming a *great* entrepreneur. He added business management classes at Rice to his workload and learned how to create an LLC for the launch of a start-up he was planning.

The investment paid off: in 2017, Carlos entered his business concept—introducing digital taxi top displays for Smart Cities and Smart Gas in Mexico—into the Rice Launch Challenge, where his team won first place. As a result, Carlos received grant funding for his start-up. "That worked out incredibly well," said Carlos, who added that his coach's "guiding hand offered me permission to step out of my boundaries, permission to be different, and permission to do what I needed to do." Carlos not only gained the confidence to kick-start his business, but he also leveraged a leadership opportunity on campus to help other students pursue their own entrepreneurial ideas. He used his role as president of Rice's Institute of Electrical and Electronics Engineers (IEEE) to spread the message of combining innovative methods with academic subjects learned through the engineering department to create opportunities beyond the conventional, corporate career path. "There are other students out there who enjoy what they're learning but are more entrepreneurial than focused on entering the traditional workforce," explained Carlos.

Carlos was able to use his experience at the Doerr Institute to follow his own trajectory rather than pursuing either a traditional application of his degree or dropping off the radar in discouragement when his goals failed to match the expectations that others had of him. Carlos credits the coaching he received through the Doerr Institute with helping him gain the confidence he needed to develop his identity as a leader, including the ability to envision himself serving in additional leadership roles. As we noted in the previous chapter, in addition to self-categorization as a leader, leader identity also encompasses leadership self-confidence, a basic sense of self-awareness of one's strengths and weaknesses as a leader, and a willingness to lead.[61] Leader identity provides the motivational wellspring from which derives the drive to pursue the leadership opportunities that form the foundational experiences for the cultivation of leadership competencies[62] (which we'll discuss in more detail in Chapter 4).

Although Carlos graduated from Rice with an engineering degree, he viewed the insights he gained from his development experiences as being just as valuable as his degree—in particular, a fundamental awareness about his talents and abilities that gave him the confidence to pursue a career goal about which he felt passionate. In other words, he had begun to learn how to embody his own leadership "ideal self."

Carlos's metamorphosis from a confused student questioning his career direction to a confident young leader, both within the university setting and in his start-up, is a perfect example of why the Doerr Institute considers helping students cultivate a strong leader identity to be one of the most important steps in the process of leader development. As we noted in the opening of this chapter, cultivating strong leader identities in students is something that the national service academies do very well (in addition to selecting students for admission who already tend to see themselves as leaders). Indeed, before anyone can develop strong leadership skills, such as vision casting, delegation, or conflict management, they must first *believe* they are a leader (or can become one). Thus, a robust leader identity lays the necessary groundwork for subsequent leadership behaviors. Although such an identity certainly isn't sufficient for effective leadership, without it, people will not tend to grow as leaders, as they are likely to avoid taking on the responsibilities and roles within which they can practice their leadership skills, receive feedback about what they tend to do well (and not so well) as leaders, and engage in the supplemental learning experiences that they need in order to evolve.[63]

This kind of personal evolution isn't likely to "just happen" without a strategic intervention, one that provides people with feedback and self-reflection to cultivate self-awareness. As the eminent leadership scholar David Day and his colleagues wrote: "Self-reflection and integration need to be planned and strategic (i.e., intentional), as individuals may not undertake personal development activities or see their potential benefit on the job without prompting."[64] As we noted in the previous chapter, this assertion is supported by our own data at Rice University, which has shown that leader identity hardly changes at all over the four years of the average student's college career. However, this consistency in leader identity over time comes with a caveat. We identified 10 campuswide leader development opportunities available to students at Rice, in addition to a few more opportunities that are specific to students involved in particular majors, such as engineering. When we examined students who had participated in one or more of the 10 campuswide leader development opportunities, it appeared that these students had, in fact, experienced growth in their leader identities (more on these opportunities later). The graph below, which uses data from a campus-wide survey of over 3,000 undergraduates, shows leader identity levels of Rice University students from freshman to senior year as a function of whether or not they had engaged in one or more leader development programs, including working with the Doerr Institute.

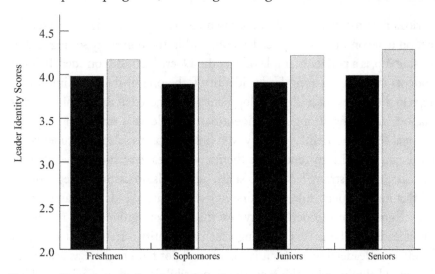

Figure 4. Changes in leader identity over time as a function of whether or not students ever engaged in any formal leader development programs on campus

As this graph shows, students who had never engaged in any of the available leader development opportunities on campus tended to have almost identical levels of leader identity from freshman to senior year.* However, the students who had engaged in at least one of the development opportunities available to them exhibited significantly stronger leader identities than did their same-level peers.

Not only did these students exhibit stronger leader identities at every level of schooling compared to their undeveloped peers, but seniors in this group now exhibited significantly stronger leader identities than freshmen did.† Although the differences in leader identity shown in Figure 4 are not exact-

---

* A formal test of the difference between freshmen and seniors in the no-LD group (which includes over 900 students) was not statistically significant, $p > .80$.
† For readers with a statistical background, we conducted a 2-way factorial ANOVA on leader identity, using year in school and whether or not students had participated in at least one leader development program as the predictor variables. This ANOVA revealed main effects of both year in school, $F(3, 3024) = 5.06, p < .005$, and leader development participation, $F(1, 3024) = 123.6, p < .001$. Furthermore, the simple effect of leader development participation was statistically significant within each year in school (all $ps < .01$), as was the difference between freshmen and senior leader identity in the subgroup of students who had engaged in at least one leader development experience ($p < .02$).

ly dramatic, they do suggest that participating in formal leader development opportunities might be beneficial, at least when it comes to the outcome of leader identity. The data shown in Figure 4 don't indicate *which* leader development experiences might be responsible for any changes in leader identity, of course, which is a subject that we will return to shortly.

Additional research by other scholars has helped shape the Doerr Institute's focus on leader identity. For instance, a study by Darja Miscenko, Hannes Guenter, and David Day mapped changes in leader identity over a seven-week leader development program.[65] The researchers found that "changes in leader identity are associated with, and potentially shaped by, changes in leadership skills across time."[66] In other words, identity leads to experience and skill development, which then feed back into and enhance identity. Knowing that the way people think of themselves as leaders can change based on their experiences supports the idea of implementing leader development programs that facilitate growth in leader identity. Herminia Ibarra, professor of leadership and learning at INSEAD, echoed this notion in her book *Act Like a Leader, Think Like a Leader*.[67] She adds that this cyclical process occurs within a *social context*, a fact that research shows is fundamental to identity development. Specifically, she argues,

> When we act like a leader…people see us behaving as leaders and confirm as much. The social recognition and reputation that develop over time with repeated demonstrations of leadership create conditions for what psychologists call *internalizing* a leadership identity—coming to see oneself as a leader and seizing more and more opportunities to behave accordingly.[68]

Turning the causal arrow in the other direction, Katherine L. Yeager of Texas A&M University and Jamie L. Callahan of Drexel University conducted a study focused on the development of leader identity among young adult leaders.[69] Noting that previous research by Bruce Avolio and Gretchen Vogelgesang found that "most developmental activities begin too late in life to make an optimal difference in a leader's behavior,"[70] Yeager and Callahan's study featured young adult leaders practicing leadership during their later years of high school. The researchers found that four main factors influenced the young adult participants' leader identity development: relationships, leading by example, developing leadership authenticity, and being motivated to lead. The researchers noted, "Identity development is *an outcome based on the experiences* that affirmed, validated, and challenged the young adult leaders in this study" (emphasis added).[71] So, in sum, leader identity appears to help facilitate engagement in leadership roles, and the experience of leading within these roles helps to shape subsequent leader identity.

Besides the broad, high-level evidence of differences in leader identity associated with student engagement in leader development opportunities, shown in Figure 4, what evidence do we have that leader identity responds to a specific training intervention? Could it be, for instance, that students who engage in various leader development opportunities around campus are simply higher in leader identity to begin with, before they ever participate in any leadership-oriented programs (a matter of selection bias)?

As we've noted already, the Doerr Institute has given a leader identity measure to all students on campus at Rice University (shown in Figures 2 and 4), and this survey provides a powerful source of comparative data from the student body. In addition, students complete this same measure before and after they work with a professional leadership coach through the Institute. This approach provides a common outcome metric across students, which is especially valuable for evaluating the impact of leadership coaching, in which people decide for themselves what specific leadership goals to work on with their coaches. Because the campus-wide survey is given to students in the middle of the fall semester, roughly six weeks after coaching has commenced for students engaged in our leadership coaching program, we can use the data from the campus-wide survey to capture average, "mid-coaching" levels of leader identity (compared to "pre-coaching" and "post-coaching" levels) for students who were working with a leadership coach, and we can contrast these levels with those of students at Rice who had never worked with a leadership coach (essentially, compressing the four bars shown back in Figure 2 into a single bar).

As the graph below shows, the average pre-coaching level of students' leader identities was just slightly below the campus-wide (non-coached) leader identity average. This difference shows that students who engage in leadership coaching with us are not a select group of students who already have unusually strong leader identities. However, after working with a professional leadership coach over the course of a semester, these students grow substantially in their leader identities. Bear in mind that coached and non-coached students are virtually identical, on average, in terms of all major demographic variables we have ever measured, such as gender, international status, first-generation college status, and major, as well as GPA and basic personality.

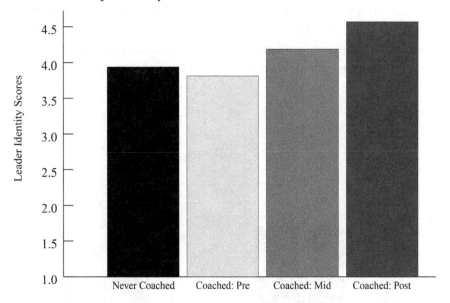

Figure 5. Changes in leader identity before, during, and after a semester of leadership coaching compared to leader identity among students who had never been coached

A careful reader might wonder whether we have reason to believe these self-reported changes in leader identity are truly meaningful. After all, students come to us desiring to develop as leaders, which indicates their intrinsic motivation to grow in this domain. Should we be surprised that, after pouring themselves into the coaching process and giving up their valuable time outside of classes, internships, and student employment to work with a coach, they tell us they feel more confident to lead, more aware of their leadership strengths and weaknesses, and more likely to define themselves as capable of leading? Perhaps not. Because this is a legitimate and important question, we have sought external corroboration for the self-reported pre-post changes in leader identity that we have found in our coaching program.

One such source of corroboration comes from the professional coaches we use. Across several semesters, we asked coaches to nominate the students who had exhibited the most (and the least) growth during the semester in which they had worked with them. Keep in mind that these coaches did not have access to the students' pre-post leader identity scores. Thus, the coaches were essentially "blind" to our hypothesis and to the student changes that we were attempting to validate. What the coaches told us provided strong validation of the pre-post changes we had measured. As shown in the graph below, the average change in students' leader identities from before to after a semester of coaching matched the levels of growth that coaches separately told us they had observed in students.*

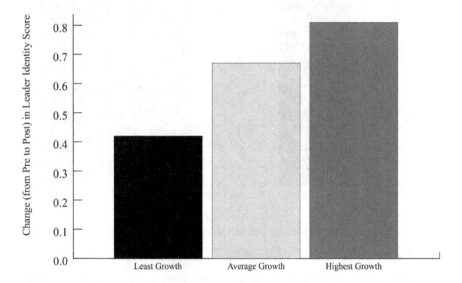

Figure 6. Average amount of leader identity change among students nominated by coaches for exhibiting low, average, or high degrees of growth

We will have more to say about measured changes in students, both with respect to leader identity and other types of outcomes, in Chapter 5. For now, however, we will simply offer the conclusion that significant changes in leader identity are possible to observe and to corroborate through external sources of observation following an intentional, carefully executed developmental initiative. Outside of such an initiative, though, leader identity does not appear to change very much just with time alone.

---

* Specifically, in a sample of more than 260 students, the changes (from before to after coaching) in leader identity that we measured in students were significantly different across the three groups defined by coaches' nominations, according to a one-way analysis of variance, $F(2, 262) = 5.80, p = .003$. Although even the group that coaches believed had grown the least still showed significant increases in leader identity after a semester of coaching, these students did not exhibit as much change in leader identity as did the group that the coaches identified as having grown the most.

The Affective Component of Leader Development: Emotional Intelligence

We've argued that having a strong leader identity is critical as a foundation for developing as a leader. Without the ability to see oneself as a leader, along with at least a modicum of confidence and self-awareness of one's leadership strengths and weaknesses, a person is unlikely to enter into the roles and responsibilities within which true leader competencies can be cultivated through practice and feedback. Our argument is, thus, that having a strong leader identity is a necessity for developing as a leader. But it's not sufficient, we would add. In order to succeed in any leadership role, a person needs to have a reasonably high level of the social-emotional skills often referred to as "emotional intelligence," a term coined by researchers Peter Salovey and John Mayer back in 1990.[72] Emotional intelligence is thought to be a critical ingredient in effective leadership; without it, a person with a strong leader identity might enter into a leadership role but be more likely to fail. Failure serves as negative feedback, which then might be internalized as evidence that the person doesn't really have what it takes to lead well. If this message is internalized, leader identity erodes, and future opportunities to lead might be avoided. Because of this, we would argue that a sufficient level of emotional intelligence, or EQ, is another necessary ingredient in developing as a leader.

A great deal has been written about the concept of emotional intelligence. Not all of it is of much value. One needn't look far to find grandiose claims about the importance of emotional intelligence for leadership (or virtually every other form of achievement we might be interested in, for that matter). For instance, some prominent spokespeople for EQ have argued that it completely overshadows intellectual ability, or IQ, in predicting successful leadership.[73]

In the academic realm, EQ skeptics are probably more common than EQ supporters. Part of the reason for this imbalance, we think, is the label itself. Psychologists have studied general cognitive ability (typically referred to in academic circles as "g," rather than IQ) for over 100 years. More has probably been written about IQ than just about any other subject in the field of psychology. We know about the structure of IQ, how to measure it reliably, and what proportion of the differences in IQ among human beings can be attributed to genetics. We understand that genes related to intelligence can interact with environments, and we even know something about how the measurement of IQ can go awry when people are subject to strong social stereotypes about their cognitive abilities.[74] Above all and most relevantly, we know that when it comes to leadership—both in terms of emergence and effectiveness—IQ matters.

For this and other reasons, when an academic who has studied IQ hears the word "intelligence," an entire suite of knowledge structures is activated, including a long history within the field of psychology.[75] But the schemas associated with this history do not apply very well to EQ. Without getting too deep into the weeds of statistics and complex, esoteric concepts, we would simply say that the structure of EQ, when it's measured, does not mimic the structure of IQ. There isn't an understood, biological underpinning to EQ like there is to IQ, even though recent work suggests that EQ *is* partly genetic.[76] Thus, when people suggest that "EQ trumps IQ" as a predictor of leadership abilities, academics scoff at the notion. "After all," the typical intelligence researcher might say, "there's really no such thing as EQ. It's not even a *thing*, so it can't be a *better* thing than IQ, which is most definitely a thing." And they have a point. The label "emotional intelligence" really is problematic, from an academic point of view, because of all that the word "intelligence" implies. (Although, to be fair, if researchers early on had called EQ something like "social-emotional skills," it's likely the concept would have struggled to gain an audience, so we might not still be talking about it today. Labels can make a big difference.)

To make matters worse, measures of EQ have proven to be more than a little problematic. To oversimplify the story just a bit here, there are basically two types of EQ measures in the world: performance-based measures, which demand that people demonstrate their levels of EQ across a series of distinct behavioral tasks, and self-report measures, which ask people a series of questions about themselves that they answer more like they would a personality test.[77] There is no academic consensus on which is the "right" way to measure EQ among researchers who accept the premise that EQ is a legitimate construct to be measured in the first place. Each approach to measuring EQ has its pros and its cons. In general, though, the personality-styled approach has resulted in some of the strongest evidence to date of the ability of EQ to predict successful job performance, both among leaders and followers.[78]

Unfortunately, as some critics have noted, this approach is likely to mix a degree of actual personality into the EQ cocktail, which makes scores from measures that take this approach difficult to interpret.[79] If EQ scores based on such measures end up predicting which leaders are most successful, independent of IQ scores, what does this really mean? Does it mean that EQ is truly important for leaders, or might it simply mean that personality matters, which we've known for a long time?

To be clear, there are studies that have attempted to tease apart these complex issues. Across the relevant literature, the best evidence to date[80] seems to indicate that IQ is one of the strongest known differentiators between effective and ineffective leaders, as well as who emerges as a leader within a sample of people. Personality makes a much weaker contribution to separating the leadership "wheat" from the "chaff." EQ, depending on how it's measured, typically falls somewhere between the two (albeit somewhat closer to the personality end than the IQ end).[*81]

Such a conclusion about the relative strength of EQ is a far cry from the bold claims about the importance of EQ, and it certainly makes for a less sensational headline than something like "EQ Beats IQ When It Comes to What Makes a Leader Great." Nonetheless, the evidence to date makes us willing to stipulate that IQ is a necessary element of effective leadership and that EQ isn't *more* important than—or even *as* important as—IQ. Someone who is as dumb as a bag of rocks is not going to be an effective leader. Perhaps we all can think of a few people who have somehow managed to attain powerful leadership positions but who, nonetheless, appear to lack the intellectual prowess to fulfill the responsibilities of their positions. Cognitive ability matters a lot.

But can't we also think of plenty of leaders who have lots of IQ but lack much in the way of EQ? Consider for a moment the best leaders you have ever known personally. What made them such good leaders? We've posed this very question to hundreds of professionals, and every time we do, the percentage that references something in the realm of IQ (e.g., technical skills, general smarts) is under 10 percent. Most often, it's even under 5 percent. What makes up the other 90–95 percent of people's responses falls under the broad category of EQ. The reason for this stark contrast, by the way, is almost certainly that, to rise to the level of being a leader, most people have to pass through multiple IQ filters, starting with the filters associated with a college degree and followed, perhaps, by graduate school. So, the strong leaders who come to mind when we ask people this ques-

* A 2010 meta-analysis by Joseph and Newman strongly supports this view, although how strongly EQ is related to personality and cognitive ability depends partly on how EQ is measured.

tion are likely to all have high IQ. But it's their high EQ that makes them stand out from leaders with equal power and authority (and IQ) who are, nonetheless, ineffective.

This whole discussion about IQ and EQ is great, you might be thinking, but so what? IQ can't be changed very much,[82] so knowing someone's IQ is only good for filtering people in or out of roles that require intellectual ability. Is that also true of EQ? Can EQ be changed? The good news is that it can.

Let's return briefly to the academic controversy over whether EQ is "real" in the same way that IQ is. When academics argue against the EQ construct, they are almost always arguing about the misuse of the label "intelligence," or they are arguing about the artificial combination of a host of social-emotional skills into a singular concept.* The latter argument is something like taking an assortment of fruits, vegetables, breads, and canned goods; sticking them together in a sack; and proclaiming them to be groceries. No one will resent this label, but they will also recognize the uniqueness of each element within the grocery sack. They will understand this "grocery" label to be a very broad, loose category that doesn't actually tell them much about what, exactly, is in the sack. Likewise, the academic EQ skeptics don't like the EQ label—akin to the label of "groceries" in this analogy—but that doesn't mean they don't believe in the validity of each of the components that make up the EQ concept. Analogously, they might not believe that the label "groceries" tells them very much, but they do believe in the reality of fruits, vegetables, bread, and canned goods.

For example, if self-awareness is one of the core elements of EQ, as most EQ models claim, even the most ardent "EQ deniers" won't suggest that there's no such thing as self-awareness. Likewise, critics will agree that empathy—the ability to understand and feel the emotions of others—is a real ability that differs between people. The same is true for self-control, emotional regulation, or interpersonal skills. We could continue down the list of characteristics that EQ supporters say make up the EQ construct. Each is valid, and *each one of them can change*. Even if we revert back to measuring these abilities as aspects of EQ, research shows that EQ scores are responsive to structured interventions.[83] What all of this means is that the features that make up emotional intelligence are subject to change, just as leader identity is.

---

* Scholars Dana Joseph and Daniel Newman (2010) actually used the phrase, "grab bag" of loosely connected concepts (p. 59).

It's also worth noting that leader identity and emotional intelligence are somewhat connected, at least conceptually. Recall that we have measured students' leader identities not only in terms of how they define themselves but also in terms of their levels of self-confidence in leading, their willingness to step into leadership roles, and their awareness of their strengths and weaknesses as leaders. So, at least with respect to the element of self-awareness, leader identity and emotional intelligence seem related. Despite this modest connection, though, we would argue that leader identity and the skills and abilities that comprise emotional intelligence are complementary, particularly for the development of new leaders. Where identity provides the impetus for stepping into a leadership role and taking on the responsibilities inherent in that role, emotional intelligence provides the soft skills needed to succeed in that role, which then reinforces leader identity the way that success in school reinforces a student's academic self-concept. Alone, neither is sufficient, but together, they make a powerful combination. Programs designed to develop people as leaders ought to focus on both of these dimensions.

The primary way that the Doerr Institute addresses emotional intelligence in its programs is by giving every student who works with a leadership coach a measure of their emotional intelligence, the EQ-i 2.0 (which stands for Emotional Quotient Inventory, version 2).*[84] Students receive a formal report of their EQ-i scores, which they discuss with their coaches in their first coaching session. Coaches enourage students to consider how their scores fit (or don't fit) with how they see themselves and to solicit additional feedback about their EQ strengths and weaknesses from people who know them well. Together, these multiple sources of feedback about their EQ, combined with self-reflection and discussion with their coach, help form the foundation of their coaching experience and set them on their path of growth as leaders.

Conclusion

Systematic, empirical data provide evidence for the importance of cultivating leader identity and social-emotional skills in students. Students' own experiences complement these data. For instance, remember Carlos, the entrepreneurial engingeering student who we mentioned earlier in

---

* The EQ-i 2.0 is a measure of emotional intelligence based on the original research of Reuven Bar-On and is distributed by Multi-Health Systems of Canada, https://storefront.mhs.com/collections/eq-i-2-0.

this chapter. Carlos described the personal insights he gained through his EQ report as one of the most helpful aspects of his work with the Doerr Institute. While attending an engineering conference, he carried with him a copy of his EQ report. "Whenever I felt like I was either losing focus or wasn't doing enough to advance my goals, I sat down and looked through it." His EQ report helped remind him of his strengths, such as building social capital and initiating projects, as well as areas for growth opportunities, such as asking for help, maintaining focus, and following through on his commitments and goals.

Similarly, another student Anthony, described a challenge he faced prior to working with the Doerr Institute: grappling with the common myth that great leaders are simply born that way, rather than developed and trained. Anthony called his belief that the quality of assertiveness was just inherently a part of one's character his "biggest mental roadblock"—a roadblock to his leader identity that he was able to circumvent, with help from his coach, by the end of the program. "I was stuck in a rut for the longest time, being either too assertive or not assertive at all, which are both qualities that can hamper your effectiveness as a leader," said Anthony. "Now that I have found more of a balance, I feel more complete as a leader."

Like many of his fellow students, Anthony credits feedback on the EQ-i, in conjunction with coaching, as being critical to his development and described the instrument's role in increasing his self-knowledge as invaluable. The assessment brought to light areas of both strength and weakness that he previously didn't know even existed, much less that they were important qualities for leaders.

Although it is difficult to replicate the frequency and depth of feedback provided to students like Ronaldo at the national military academies, as we described at the beginning of this chapter, Carlos and Anthony's experience with feedback on the EQ-i is typical of the experiences described by other students we have worked with over the last few years. Despite all of the academic feedback that students at Rice (and other institutions of higher education) receive during their undergraduate years, few, if any, ever receive the sort of personal, developmental feedback as students that midshipmen like Ronaldo receive every single semester at the USNA. Thus, even a simple report like the one accompanying the EQ-i can be powerful.

In addition to assertiveness, Anthony also scored low in self-regard and optimism, characteristics that tend to be strongly linked with one another.

> It posed...a tall task, at first, for me to work on improving things such as my self-worth and optimism. However, looking back at the progress I have made from my initial start at the Doerr Institute, I feel that the knowledge of the specific steps I can take to improve my leadership has been the most valuable information I have gained, and it has allowed me to develop into not just a better leader but also a better person.

In this chapter, we have discussed the foundational concepts of leader identity and emotional intelligence, and we have described how the Doerr Institute addresses these concepts within some of its developmental work with students. We continue this discussion in the next chapter, which focuses on the development of more specific leader competencies that build on these foundational concepts.

FOR REFLECTION: Is Your Program Prioritizing the Fundamentals?

Before students can develop meaningful leadership skills and behaviors, they must first self-identify as a leader and cultivate a set of basic, social-emotional skills. Once people have done so, they can begin to develop more specific leadership skills. Without a strong leader identity, students are unlikely to begin this process of skill development. Do you give any attention to helping students develop these internal qualities? Consider the following challenge questions below:

1. Does your leader development program use an assessment tool during onboarding to help students understand their strengths and weaknesses, so they will know what they want to leverage and what they want to change?
2. Do you gather pre- and post-intervention data to help determine the extent to which your work with students has an impact on fundamental outcomes, such as leader identity?
3. Does your leadership program conflate leader development with career development?
4. Does your program filter and recruit only the strongest student leaders, or is it designed to attract and develop all students, even students who might begin with weaker leader identities?

Chapter 4

LEADING WITH SKILL:

Building Leader Competencies on the Foundation of Identity and Emotional Intelligence

Leader identity is partially about feeling confident enough to envision oneself as a leader. But if that heightened confidence isn't reflected in the types of behavior changes that underlie effective leadership, then it isn't particularly valuable to either individuals or organizations, and it might be little more than a self-serving delusion, akin to the infamous Dunning-Kruger Effect.[85] It isn't enough to simply help students develop their leader identity and the building blocks of emotional intelligence. The next stage of the process must address how students can actively transform their desire to lead into specific leadership competencies.

Practicing leadership skills is critical at this stage. As Marshall Goldsmith, author of *What Got You Here Won't Get You There*, writes,

> Becoming a better leader is a process, not an event. Nobody ever changed just by going to a training session. They got better by doing what they learned in the program. And that "doing," by definition, involves follow-up. Follow-up turns changing for the better into an ongoing process—not only for you but for everyone involved.[86]

As described in Chapter 3, emotional intelligence (EQ) plays an important role in this process. Helping students gain self-awareness about particular strengths and weaknesses in fundamental social-emotional skills is a critical first step to igniting change and transforming behaviors that might be holding them back from successfully leading. But what happens next—how students actually leverage the new awareness gained from the EQ-i's results—is just as important to the process of developing students as leaders. As Jim Kouzes and Barry Posner note in their book *Learning*

Leadership, almost everyone has at least some leadership capability.[87] The challenge, then, isn't about finding the "right" students with leadership potential but, rather, helping every student learn how to practice effective leadership behaviors more often.

Inhabiting Leadership

Remember Carlos from the last chapter? He was the Rice engineering student who strengthened his leader identity through Doerr's program in order to carve his own unique path as a leader and entrepreneur. This didn't happen overnight but through a series of steps leading to behavior changes that took place over the course of his semester of being coached and beyond. After Carlos had gained insights into his own EQ-related strengths and weaknesses, he then worked one-on-one with his coach to move that new understanding out of a theoretical framework and into specific leadership actions.

Gaining new competencies helped him transition from a confused and frustrated engineering student into the leader of his own business. That experience also helped him develop leadership skills as he shared his knowledge with other engineering students in his department. With the guidance of his coach, Carlos leveraged the insights from the EQ-i not only to see himself differently as someone with leadership potential but also to truly become different by activating that potential to reach his goals. While continuing to build on the strengths that the EQ-i had identified, such as project initiation, he also began taking concrete steps to shift his behaviors, such as asking for help, maintaining his focus, and following through on his commitments. By changing what he did little by little, Carlos morphed from merely thinking about himself as a leader into actually stepping into a leadership role in his area of interest (entrepreneurship), winning first place in the Rice Launch Challenge in 2017, and then using those grant funds to seed his start-up.

Carlos's experience serves as a great example of how a student can move from self-identifying as a leader to exhibiting and practicing the necessary competencies of leaders in the real world—*inhabiting* leadership, rather than merely thinking about it in the abstract. People must take specific steps to realize success in this arena; research on "implementation intentions" has shown that this process isn't likely to happen without effort and intentionality.[88]

Likewise, a recent study on personality change by Nathan Hudson and colleagues underscored how critical it is that people take action in order to change; it also noted the profound insufficiency of simply pondering the ways in which they would like to be different from how they are.[89] Most of us know this from personal experience with "goals" that turned out to be little more than fantasies. Although reflecting on a desired future and articulating a goal to pursue that future are important first steps in the process of change, they are not enough. Hudson and colleagues began their study by asking nearly 400 participants what aspects of their personalities they wished were different. Each week after the study began, the researchers sent participants short lists of exercises from which they could choose to work. These exercises were designed by personality experts to help people practice altering their habits of thought, feeling, and behavior in order to produce and reinforce desired changes. As Hudson and his colleagues showed, over a period of 15 weeks, participants in their study made progress toward their desired self-changes only if they actively engaged in the change exercises that they had selected. Selecting the exercises, like articulating their self-change goals, was not enough. Moreover, those who had articulated a desired change and selected change exercises but didn't actually work on their chosen exercises showed a modest tendency to change in the opposite direction as their stated goal.[90] Desiring change is clearly not enough when it comes to self-transformation.

Consistent with this finding, an effective leader development program should make sure that students don't get stuck at the leader identity stage with an unfulfilled desire to change and grow as leaders. Rather, students should move intentionally and concretely from vision and identity to execution and ability, with professional guidance on how to implement new skills and develop specific leader competencies. For us, this shift from an abstract desire to actualization begins with the Leader Development Plan (or LDP), which is composed of three parts that build sequentially, moving from abstract self-reflection to explicit action planning (see Appendix 1). On their LDPs, students begin with a personal overview of themselves and their leadership-related values, as well as where they see themselves as leaders at present. Part of this honest self-inventory of their current selves involves reflecting on the results of their EQ-i report and soliciting additional feedback from other people who know them well. Next, students reflect on what kind of leader they would ideally like to be. Envisioning this leadership ideal self is designed to help students create an intrinsically inspiring mental model that will motivate them to do all of the difficult work involved in self-transformation.

The importance of this internal mental model can hardly be overstated. How many people make New Year's resolutions that they never actually achieve? Perhaps one of the reasons for this common self-development failure is that so many such resolutions aren't all that inspiring. Indeed, many resolutions for personal change reflect people's sense of what they are *supposed* to be, do, or look like (what researchers refer to as people's "ought self"),*[91] rather than who they truly and deeply *want* to become. In other words, many personal goals contain some kind of "what" but are often missing an intrinsically motivated "why." The powerful "why" of effective personal development is frequently found in a person's ideal self. Rarely is it found in extrinsically motivated goals derived from an abstract prototype of someone else's vision.

In *Switch: How to Change Things When Change Is Hard*, brothers Chip and Dan Heath underscore this point beautifully by drawing upon decades worth of social science research on changing personal habits, organizations, and social systems.[92] They borrow a metaphor from another social scientist, Jonathan Haidt, in which the human mind is pictured as a rider atop a large elephant.[93] The rider represents a person's prefrontal cortex, that part of the brain in which complex analyses, self-regulation, and planning take place. The rider is smart and capable of great feats of logic and insight. However, the rider is, at the end of the day, a tiny person perched upon a great beast, and the best the rider can do is nudge and prod the elephant to get it to go where he wants it to go. The elephant represents the more emotionally oriented limbic system in the brain, a primitive and powerful mental system where desire lives and from which motivation springs. The elephant is large and powerful and really only knows what it *wants*. Although it is able to take *some* direction from the rider, it is not itself capable of logic or reasoning.

Heath and Heath note that for a person to engage in the difficult process of change, motivating the elephant is critical.[94] Most of us can't simply reason our way to changing our diet, engaging in rigorous exercise, or completing that college degree we never finished. If we could, everyone would be healthy, fit, and well educated. In reality, most Americans are

---

*Classic research by psychologist Torry Higgins distinguishes the "actual self" from the "ideal self" and the "ought self," with important emotional consequences related to gaps between the actual and ideal selves and between the actual and ought selves.

overweight or obese, cardiovascular disease is one of the leading causes of death, and only about 30 percent of us finish college. Thus, creating a compelling vision from which we can draw deep inspiration is key to successfully motivating the process of change, as well as keeping that level of motivation high. Heath and Heath refer to this vision as a "destination postcard."[95] We suggest that an effective leader development program should take this idea of a destination postcard—or a person's leadership best self—seriously and have students create their own vision of what they want to achieve and who they want to be. This vision cannot be imposed externally. It must be intrinsic, non-coerced, and not handed to them as passive recipients.

We find that, when working with students to imagine their leadership best self, many of them have never actually been asked to articulate who they want to be as a leader. Students at Rice and other highly selective schools don't get admitted merely on charm and good looks. Getting into an elite university like Rice is predicated on, for some students, nearly two decades of planning and programming supported and guided by enthusiastic parents, dedicated K–12 teachers, and well-meaning college counselors and consultants. But very little of this planning and programming involves having students envision and express what *they* want and who *they* most want to be. Students often arrive at elite universities conditioned to be very good followers and high achievers. But learning to lead requires inhabiting a new identity with different skills and experiences. This growth arc involves moving from what developmental psychologist Robert Kegan calls a "socialized mind" to a more independent, "self-authoring mind," such that students take their growth into their own hands and take full ownership over their own development.[96]

When students sit down with a professional coach to work on their personalized leader development plan, there are often awkward moments of silence in which students are forced to begin the inward journey of discovery that allows them to create a vision for their leadership best self. They are often frustrated with their coach at this stage in the process. The feedback they give us indicates that many of them want their coach to simply direct them and tell them what to do. As we noted in Chapter 2, though, the professionally trained coach knows better. The coach's job is to ask and to listen and then to ask some more. The coach's job is not to tell or to teach or to mentor or to consult, for the most part. But the struggle created by the coach's trained reticence proves its value in the long run, when the intrinsically derived goals that students set for themselves, inspired by their imagined best self, take flight and students begin to see change and progress. A small number of students (about 2 percent) drop out after their first session with their coach. Those who come back for a second session almost always (> 96 percent of the time in our program) complete an entire semester's worth of coaching (typically five sessions), however, and 97 percent of students tell us that they made meaningful progress toward their goals by the end of five sessions.

To achieve this level of success, though, it's important to draw upon what we know about effective goal setting from decades worth of research—or, to return to the metaphor of the rider and the elephant, not to forget about what the rider does best. Thus, on their leader development plans, students move from articulating an intrinsically inspiring vision for who they want to be and what they want to achieve to creating a defined action plan complete with a reflection on what resources they will need to achieve this plan, what roadblocks they are likely to encounter, and with defined markers of success (so they will know if they are making progress). This plan becomes the framework for ongoing engagement and feedback between the coach and student.

In a sense, the LDP establishes a student's leadership objectives and the key results that mark the achievement of those objectives, which are reminiscent of the "objectives and key results" approach to goal setting that John Doerr has popularized in his bestselling book, *Measure What Matters*.[97] Examples of some of the most common leadership goals that students choose to work on are shown in the graph below. It is, we suspect, not an accident that these common goals overlap with key elements of emotional intelligence, which we described in the last chapter.

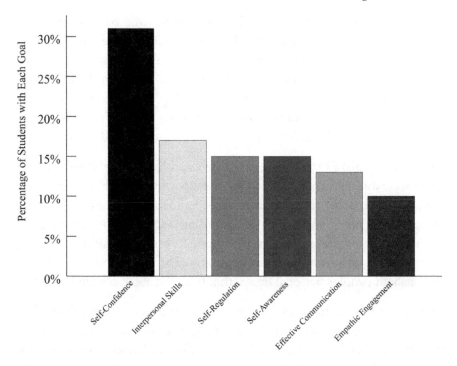

Figure 7. The most common goals pursued by students involved in one-on-one coaching

One Size Fits None

Students launch their leadership journey from many different starting points, depending on their existing skills, backgrounds, preferences, and personalities. Some students have relatively mature visions for where they would like to go in life and how they want to give back and make an impact (frequent core values for students from so-called "Generation Z"). Others have little sense of what their futures hold or what they even want them to hold. They are more like the teenaged protagonist (played by John Cusack) in the 1989 pop film *Say Anything*. He doesn't know what he wants to do, but he knows he doesn't want to sell anything, make anything, or buy anything. Furthermore, students at top universities in the U.S. hail from cultures all around the world. Some plan to remain in the U.S. after they graduate, but many plan to return home to their culture of origin.

The variety among students who seek leader development continually excites us, and it also challenges us to resist slotting students into any kind of one-size-fits-all mold. For example, MiYoung is an Asian-American woman who didn't see herself as a leader until she worked with her coach and realized she had a limiting belief that wealthy white students were better positioned and more respected as leaders. She had not been exposed to strong role models who inspired her to believe that an Asian woman could aspire or rise to a position of leadership. As MiYoung strengthened her leader identity, she determined that the leadership behaviors she needed to work on included improving her confidence and assertiveness.

Likewise, Jonathan came to the Institute as an introvert who believed his value was working behind the scenes in supporting roles. His coach could see how capable and effective he could be as a leader and helped Jonathan recognize the need to become more intentional about his behavior regarding relationship building and reaching out to others, including investing time in others outside of team meetings or group projects and remembering to ask about people's personal lives rather than just about academic matters.

In contrast to Jonathan, Hannah was an international student from Germany and a self-described perfectionist. She was already a leader on campus, but her tendency was to take everything on herself and do it "just right," which resulted in her feeling perpetually stressed out and stretched thin. Hannah, together with her coach, decided to work on building her delegation and team-leading skills.

This small sampling of emerging leaders that we see at the Doerr Institute shows why the traditional, one-size-fits-all approach that many universities take to leadership development is doomed to fail—MiYoung, Jonathan, and Hannah exemplify how each student comes to the table with different strengths, as well as unique areas needing development from a leadership perspective. To give them all identical training rather than addressing their specific needs would be ineffective, just as imposing a strict, universal definition of some ideal leader prototype would be both insensitive and culturally inappropriate for many (if not most) of them. These problems highlight the value of taking a more individualized approach to leader development, including (but not limited to) one-on-one coaching and student self-selection into training that meets their contextually driven needs and personal goals. Of course, taking an individualized approach can make measuring outcomes challenging, but social scientists tend to get energized by that kind of challenge.

Such an individualized approach tends to run completely counter to the culture and norms of academic institutions, which often determine the classes they will offer based on the desires of faculty members rather than the unique needs of students. After all, the faculty are the experts, right? Because what these experts know how to do is teach classes, leader development most often takes the form of leadership education (teaching *about* leadership) rather than leader development (training students to become effective leaders). As noted in Chapter 1, because faculty are typically rewarded based on their teaching and scholarship, rather than the extent to which they develop students as leaders, there is no reason for anyone to expect these broad trends to ever change, unless universities decide to take a different approach to leader development.

To enhance the capacity of students as leaders, universities should focus their efforts on practicing the behaviors associated with effective leading, not simply learning about leadership theories. Such an approach also reflects the fundamentals of Jim Kouzes and Barry Posner's *Learning Leadership*,[98] which emphasizes that to become exemplary leaders, people need to not only believe that they can lead and aspire to excel (cognitive and motivational processes), but they must also *challenge* themselves to enter into leadership roles, *engage* support within those roles, and *practice* deliberately to develop the skills needed to be effective (behavioral processes).

Leader Competencies

A critical component of the Doerr Institute's overarching mission is to prepare emerging leaders to lead with the competencies necessary to be effective. The concept of "leader competencies"—defined by the Society for Human Resource Management as "leadership skills and behaviors that contribute to superior performance"—is central to our thinking about what it means to develop students as leaders.[99] We want them to cultivate strong identities as leaders, with the confidence and awareness that undergird a healthy identity as a leader, and we want them to grow in their social-emotional skills (i.e., their emotional intelligence). But, upon the foundation of these cognitive and emotional characteristics, we also want them to build a powerful set of behavioral competencies that research shows distinguish strong and effective leaders from weak, ineffective ones.

While leadership behaviors can be uniquely expressed from one person to the next (as is the case with leader identity), we believe that it's nonetheless wise to identify a set of empirically validated competencies that will help students become the leaders they wish to be. We have derived such a list from the work of other pioneers in the field of leadership research and development, such as Michael Lombardo and Robert Eichinger,[100] whose work formed the foundation of management consulting firm Korn Ferry's 38 Global Competency Framework, the Korn Ferry Leadership Architect™.[101] Korn Ferry's framework divides leadership competencies into four factors (thought, results, people, and self), with 12 thematic groups under each of these headings to describe different types of competencies, including making complex decisions, taking initiative, influencing people, and being authentic.

As Korn Ferry notes, "For development to make a lasting difference, people must be clear on what skill or behavior they need to improve, be motivated to make the change, and know what steps to take." They add that the use of leader competencies can provide "ideas and strategies on how to improve where you need to be stronger or work around a need so that you can be as effective as possible."[102] They emphasize the importance of bringing both insight and motivation to the process—the exact approach that the Doerr Institute uses by beginning our program with the self-insights from the emotional intelligence assessment (the EQ-i 2.0) and a focus on leader identity as precursors to effective competency development.

We reviewed the published Korn Ferry competencies and selected 21 core competencies that we view as having particular relevance to early-stage student leaders. This list, while not intended to be exhaustive or definitive, provides students with a starting point to help them identify potential areas for development and represents a wide range of basic competencies. While the 21 competencies are listed and figured below, Appendix 2 additionally includes a brief description of each leader characteristic. We should emphasize that we never insist that students work on any particular competencies from this list. It is not designed to be prescriptive but rather descriptive. As is the case with the EQ-i results, the 21 core leader competencies can serve as an impetus for goal creation for students who want to grow as leaders but struggle to articulate a specific goal. We've found that most student goals can be framed as instances of either these 21 competencies or the dimensions of the social-emotional skills found on the EQ-i. Indeed, our core leader competencies and the dimensions of emotional intelligence captured by the EQ-i have some strong conceptual overlaps.

For the sake of simplicity, we've divided the core leader competencies into five broad, rationally derived themes:

- Knowing Yourself: purposefulness, self-confidence, self-awareness

- Controlling Yourself: self-regulation, balance, decision-making, perseverence
- Growing and Flourishing: innovative thinking, love of learning, vision setting, enterprising initiative
- Being Aware of Others: cross cultural resourcefulness, ethical responsibility, empathic engagement
- Working with Others: conflict management, team building, collaboration, delegation, negotiation, development, effective communication

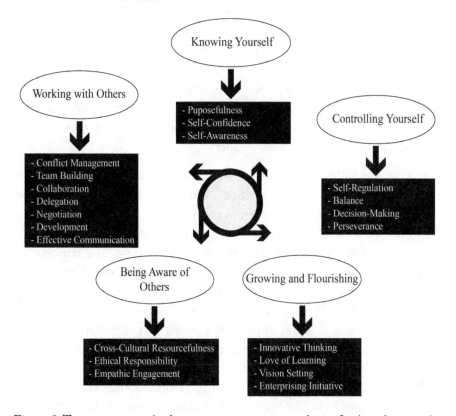

Figure 8. Twenty-one core leader competencies organized into five broad, rationally derived themes

While these competencies are all reflective of critical skills for leaders, we don't expect growth on all competencies for all students. For instance, the early stage in a professional coaching engagement involves helping students identify which leader competencies are most relevant and meaningful for them and targeting particular competencies (from this list or not) that address their individual needs. Coaches then help students assess their current state, articulate a desired future state, and outline a plan to get there, including specific actions that will help the student practice the targeted competencies. Leader competencies like those listed above are addressed in all of our work with students. For example, in our one-on-one coaching program (recall from Chapter 1 that we call this program Activation), students identify their own needs and goals and devise an action plan in concert with their coach. In our group coaching program (called Synthesis), students join a group organized according to a broad theme (e.g., communicating with confidence and clarity, leading with purpose) and then work within their group on their own specific goals. In our focused skills training program (called Catalyst), students select from a list of available training opportunities that each focus on one particular skill (e.g., how to manage conflict, how to deliver feedback), which they work on in a group setting. Finally, in CoachRICE, students experience an intensive, 60-hour training course designed to build skills to help develop others through formal coaching. Thus, all of our programs offer students the chance to develop their skills as leaders, not just their identities as leaders.

The skills and abilities that leaders need to be effective aren't set in stone, even though research has determined a limited set of common skills that seem to distinguish good leaders from mediocre ones. Rather, as leadership consultants Bob Kaplan and Robert Kaiser have noted, leaders need to be able to draw from a range of skills that vary in relevance and importance from one situation to the next in response to shifting social, economic, and global trends, as well as organizational demands, team dynamics, and the idiosyncrasies of individual contributors.[103] Thus, when we strategize about the best way to develop younger leaders, part of our strategy must involve envisioning which behaviors and skillsets will set them up for future leadership success. The World Economic Forum (WEF) has referred to the rapid shifts in business, education, government, and culture brought about by changes in technology as the "Fourth Industrial Revolution," or 4IR.[104] In the proceedings of the WEF's 2017 Annual Meeting of New Champions,[105] the Doerr Institute partnered with the China Competence Center, a think tank, and Caldwell Partners, an international executive search firm, to identify shifts in competencies that new leaders will need to master in order to adapt to the powerful social and economic trends of the next 10 to 20 years. These included the ability to work on non-hierarchical teams, build teams of follower networks, and discourage cowardice/ excessive self-interest in team members.

Promoting leader competencies to help shape leaders is supported by other research as well. Judi Brownell at Cornell University, for instance, found that organizations using a competency-based approach to leadership are better able to identify and develop future leaders.[106] A plethora of additional studies have validated that focusing on skill development and leadership competencies facilitates improved leadership, including research by Troy Mumford and colleagues on the "leadership skills strataplex."[107] The point is that while different organizations might compile different leader competency lists to help define their unique leader development frameworks,[108] no matter how they circumscribe the realm of relevant competencies, they also provide a structured, intentional framework within which behavior change could be expected to occur. Without such a framework, there is little reason to believe change will just happen on its own.[109]

Seeing the Value in Skill Development

Research illuminates certain truths about leader competency development, and actual student experiences can validate those truths just as they do for leader identity. Hayden was a Rice student who completed CoachRICE in the spring of 2018. After realizing, through his EQ-i results and subsequent work with his coach, that he lacked the ability to act authoritatively in leadership roles, he decided he wanted to develop this skill. The first step in this process was to recognize that while he had strong listening skills, he lacked decisiveness and authority in decision-making and often got bogged down in seeking total consensus from those he was leading. As his confidence grew and his leader identity solidified, Hayden's coach helped him identify behavioral changes that he could strive to master that would move him closer to his goal. Concerning his transformation, Hayden said, "I realized that [the] democratic style may not be the perfect style of leadership in every situation....One of the small goals I set for myself is to learn to interrupt people's talking at the right time." Complementing this ability, Hayden also worked on the skill of asking more effective questions of others and truly listening to their answers. These are skills that characterize professional coaches more than almost any other in their arsenal, so the training that Hayden received in coaching skills served him well in this regard—even outside of the domain of formal coaching. The skills he was developing are skills that transfer well from formal coaching to informal leading, as well as to everyday relationships.

Conclusion

In this chapter, we have discussed the importance of building upon the foundation of leader identity and emotional intelligence by helping students develop specific leadership competencies. There are many "top lists of leadership skills" that can be found, and we do not claim that our own list is the right one, or even a complete one, despite its derivation from previous research on the skills that distinguish mediocre leaders from excellent ones. To create an effective leader development program, however, you must determine what characteristics and competencies you are trying to develop in students, and then you must be sure to measure those qualities so you know if your work is successful. The critical role of measurement is the focus of the next chapter, in which we discuss the most important principles behind an effective measurement strategy and some of the preliminary evidence we have found for the effectiveness of our own programs (as well as a notable false assumption that could have dramatically affected which students we chose to develop had we not tested it with the right data).

FOR REFLECTION: Are You Training for Competence?

Once a student has begun to develop a healthy leader identity, the next step is to translate that identity into leader competencies through behavior change and skill development. Is your leadership program currently providing students with the developmental opportunities they need to become competent leaders themselves, rather than just studying what other leaders do? Consider the following challenge questions below:

1. Does your work with students stop at the cognitive stage of leader development and focus only on teaching students *about* leadership rather than helping them to practice the behavioral skills they need to lead effectively?
2. If so, how do you know? Do you have outcome measures that are sufficiently valid and reliable to drive your decisions about programming?
3. Does your program allow students the chance to focus on single leadership competencies to further develop their unique skillsets?
4. Do you offer students the opportunity to learn and practice developing their peers, as well as themselves?

Chapter 5

MEASURING UP:

The Why, How, and What of Measuring Outcomes in a Leader Development Enterprise

The Doerr Institute made an interesting discovery in our research evaluating leader development work in universities across the United States, which we described back in Chapter 1. We found that the same educational institutions that claim developing the next generation of leaders is central to their missions rarely articulate what this work involves or measure the outcomes of their ostensibly mission-critical leader development work. When any such measurement does occur, it tends to be limited to "smiley sheets"—satisfaction-based surveys filled out by students. As John Doerr has noted in his book *Measure What Matters*, organizations that say they are pursuing certain objectives but don't bother to anchor their goal pursuits with measured indicators of progress (or lack of progress) really aren't all that serious about those objectives.[110]

While satisfaction-based surveys and academic course evaluations can be a reasonable first step for measurement, they aren't sufficient on their own to evaluate whether or not a program or course of instruction is effectively increasing students' capacity to lead in a practical sense. As Keri Bennington and Tony Laffoley from the University of North Carolina at Chapel Hill noted:

> Participant feedback forms (i.e., smiley sheets) administered immediately after a learning program are no longer enough, and HR and talent management professionals are feeling the pressure to look for more solid evidence to justify the investment in their programs. This is particularly the case in leadership development programs, where the focus is often on the development of intangible skills.[111]

We would take issue with the term "intangible skills." Skills manifest in observable behaviors. Skills are always tangible, and when connected to critical leader behaviors, they are both tangible and valid. Referring to leadership qualities as "intangible" is often the first step toward giving up on measurement.

Head in the Sand

Why is there such a paucity of measurement and solid data regarding leader development in higher education? There are a number of reasons, starting with two simple ones. The first factor might be called the not-my-job syndrome. That is, in the uncommon instances in which systematic leader development programs exist, measuring leadership outcomes is typically not assigned to anyone as their primary job responsibility. Without an institutional commitment to rigorous measurement manifested in job roles, it's unlikely to happen. Second, as we noted previously, asking the hard questions about whether your program or leadership course is achieving its intended impact opens you up to the possibility that the answer is "no." That creates a vulnerability that many institutions are, understandably, not willing to embrace. When your biggest commitment is to reputation and optics rather than to a well-defined mission, measuring the results of your work can feel like a dangerous proposition.

This brings us back to another topic that we've discussed before: a lack of institutional commitment to an objective higher than the immediate costs/rewards of reputation. National rankings exacerbate this problem. On the one hand, higher education as a whole decries *U.S. News & World Report*-style rankings—yet every university pays close attention to them, too, because they recognize that they are often judged by those rankings. From their perspective, why should they open themselves up to criticism and potential losses by obtaining data (costly data, no less) that could make their institution look bad to prospective students, parents, and the general public? There are many other reasons why universities avoid measuring leader development, including administrators and staff simply not valuing empirical outcomes, not knowing exactly how to employ empirical measures effectively, and not wanting to spend already limited resources in this arena given the challenges above.

Another barrier to proper measurement in university leader development programs is that, when evaluating interventions or ideas, most people don't think like social scientists. When it comes to program design, it's rare to find someone outside of the social sciences who thinks through basic issues like reliability, validity, and the need for proper comparison groups when conducting empirical evaluations (for more on this subject, see Appendix 3). In just one example, our team recently met with a group of impressive mathematicians who have designed a math camp for minority children interested in STEM fields. But being talented in math, physics, or any similar discipline doesn't necessarily help you think like a social scientist. In fact, in this case as in many others, we found that getting people to think appropriately about defining objectives and measuring outcomes was a herculean task and one in which we did not fully succeed. And even if teams do start thinking properly about objectives and outcomes, that's only the first step. They must then put their objectives into action and commit to a process of rigorous evaluation, with the commitments of time, effort, and other resources that this process requires and the willingness to take the results of this process seriously.

Thinking Differently

Given the factors cited above, it might be understandable that universities have shied away from transparency and rigor in the measurement of programs they promote as core elements of their institutional missions. But the Doerr Institute thinks differently about measurement. By being measurement focused, we can ensure the most efficient system of development because we are able to terminate programs that don't produce meaningful outcomes. In order to know if we are, in fact, producing the outcomes that we seek, there is no alternative to rigorous measurement, whether we are in the education, non-profit, or for-profit realms. In *MIT Sloan Management Review*, Robert Gandossy and Robin Guarnieri assert:

> Human resources executives and corporate leaders across the globe find that it's simply not enough to put a leadership-training program in place or hold an annual talent review. Instead, companies must be rigorous and focused in their assessment of leadership talent, aided by tools tailored to help achieve that end....HR and business leaders also need insights into where they have succeeded in building leadership and critical talent pipelines and where there are potential risks. In short, companies need to bring a "measurement mind-set" to the often inexact process of developing the next generation of leaders.[112]

Professional leader development organizations need to be able to prove successful outcomes through data; without numbers to back up their claims, they won't likely be taken seriously by potential clients, nor should they be. Of course, some organizations do recognize the importance of measuring outcomes to prove the value of their investment in particular initiatives. But in business as well as in higher education, leader development hasn't caught up with this critical strategy. As Larry Clark, managing director of Global Learning Solutions for Harvard Business Publishing, recently emphasized, leader development and training is often approached differently from a measurement standpoint compared to other areas that seem to lend themselves to a more direct result, such as error reduction in a manufacturing plant:

> [Leader] development feels like a different animal that shouldn't be held to the same measurement standard. In some way, it feels like it's "above the law." As one learning leader once lamented to me, "They don't ask IT to measure the ROI of email, but everybody knows we still need it."[113]

And yet, as Gandossy and Gaurnieri point out:

> Most companies wouldn't go forward with a multimillion-dollar business venture without first identifying the investment goals. Nor would they jump into a deal without defining beforehand the critical action steps and expected results. Why should an investment in leadership talent be treated any differently? Engaging staff in the consideration of leadership metrics deepens the quality of company processes for specifying goals, building strengths, and seizing opportunities.[114]

Despite the clear benefits derived from measuring the impact of leadership training programs, it's not being done on a consistent basis in either academia or industry.*[115] It's time to change this state of affairs. For those interested in doing so, the rest of this chapter outlines the operating principles that guide the Doerr Institute's measurement efforts and provides some examples of ways in which we have begun to examine the impact of our own initiatives. These examples include short-term developmental

---

* Underscoring this assertion once again, Harvard's *2018 State of Leadership Development* report found that just under a quarter of surveyed organizations tried to measure the impact of their leader development initiatives. Of those who attempt to do so, satisfaction surveys are currently the most popular measurement tool, despite their clear limitations.

changes in students as well as analyses of longer-term ROI, both to students (e.g., employment) and to the university (e.g., alumni giving). Our analyses have revealed both successes and failures in the Doerr Institute's programs, not to mention some faulty intuitions on our part that would have remained built into the structure of our approach to developing students had we not maintained a self-skeptical posture and tested our assumptions empirically.

Measuring What Matters: Some Guiding Principles

Careful measurement of outcomes is central to the Doerr Institute's mission of enhancing the leadership capacity of Rice students. Paying close attention to metrics helps the Institute avoid common pitfalls that are often endemic to such endeavors, such as making decisions through groupthink and falling prey to the confirmation bias (favoring information that confirms your preexisting beliefs) or the good samaritan bias (assuming you are having the effects that you intend to have because you mean well).

The three-person, dedicated measurement team at the Doerr Institute is composed of a postdoctoral research fellow and a part-time graduate student led by a seasoned social scientist (formerly a professor of social psychology). This team operates its assessment system according to four, overarching principles, which we will describe here in broad terms and then illustrate with a series of more concrete examples.

First, in conjunction with the Doerr Institute's guiding First Principles (described in detail in the next chapter), the team measures *everything* that the Institute does. If an initiative is designed to produce a particular change in students, then that change should be quantifiable. The job of the measurement team in the Doerr Institute is to operationalize that quantity in order to empirically test the degree to which every intervention with students is having the impact it was designed to have.

Second, by keeping the measurement team independent from the leader development team, the Institute is able to minimize the natural bias that would otherwise occur if people were placed in the position of having to evaluate their own work. This independence also simplifies the process of eliminating programs that fail to produce the changes we want to see in students' leadership ability.

Third, the measurement team examines outcomes across the domains of cognition, affect, and behavior, in keeping with the purposes of each program. Some programs, for instance, are designed to modify affect, such as students' levels of self-confidence in stepping up to leadership roles. Other programs are designed to enhance specific behavioral skills, such as the ability to deliver effective feedback. The measurement team strives to fit the right outcome measures to the particular objectives of a program. Internal, psychological variables are prized neither more nor less than more overt, behavioral ones, as effective leadership depends on a wide-ranging combination of cognitive, affective, and behavioral characteristics and competencies (as noted in Chapters 3 and 4).

Fourth, and finally, the measurement team uses multiple methods to evaluate the impact of the Institute's efforts, including self-report data, observational data, and behavioral data. For example, the team measures changes in a variety of outcomes before and after a coaching or training intervention through self-report scales that capture a snapshot of where participants are at a given point in time regarding constructs such as leader identity, self-concept clarity, or sense of purpose. The team also gathers observational data from the students' peers and leadership coaches to discover whether they can see any of the growth that is shown by the self-report measures. Finally, the measurement team analyzes objective behavioral data on the formal leadership roles students inhabit to look for evidence of impact beyond all of these subjective judgments. (We will describe some more specific examples of these various approaches shortly.)

To achieve this set of aims—measuring everything, minimizing bias, assessing across the domains of cognition, affect, and behavior, and examining a wide range of outcomes using multiple measurement methods—the Doerr Institute is committed to having an independent team committed only to measurement, and this commitment currently sets the Doerr Institute apart from every other leader development initiative that we have seen in higher education. The measurement team's primary job is to bring evidence-based insights to the leader development team so they know what's working, what isn't, and how they can develop students as leaders more effectively. In doing so, the measurement team must balance the tension between being nimble enough to help people make quick decisions (sometimes in real time) and conducting measurement work that would pass muster in an academic journal, with the awareness that aspiring to this standard sometimes results in a slower, even cumbersome process.

The measurement team uses or adapts validated measures taken directly from published research whenever possible and draws upon existing academic research to home in on the right models and instruments for the Institute's programs by tuning those findings iteratively with the content of training. But when there isn't a published measure that really fits with the specific objectives of an initiative, the team develops outcome measures in-house. This process begins with clearly defining the objectives of an initiative to a level of specificity that allows the team to determine the right outcome measures. Next, it tests those outcome measures in small pilot studies that help the team to refine its approach and then examines the assessment approach at scale if the evidence from the pilot is positive. Regardless of their origin, all outcome measures undergo careful psychometric analyses throughout their use, such as assessments of internal reliability, test-retest consistency, factor structure, agreement between raters, face validity, and the like. Creating measures for some of the more abstract leader qualities that we are interested in, such as situational adaptability or interpersonal skills, can be more challenging than creating measures for more concrete outcomes, such as leader role occupancy or specific behavioral skills. Nonetheless, the process for designing, adapting, and creating the right measures to fit the objectives of a program remains consistent across our initiatives. The details might change, but good design principles remain consistent.

In some cases, the team also uses what pioneering social scientists William Shadish, Thomas Cook, and Donald Campbell called "non-dependent variables," which are outcomes that are not directly related to the content of an intervention and, therefore, should not change following the intervention.[116] This method creates a type of internal control group, sometimes called an "internal reference group,"[117] against which the outcome measures of interest can be compared. If the intervention is successful, then the outcome measures related to the intervention (the dependent variables) ought to change significantly, whereas the outcome measures unrelated to the intervention (the non-dependent variables) should not. This kind of approach is particularly useful when researchers use measures that rely on participants' self-reports and when true experimentally determined control groups are impossible or impractical.

So far, we have described in rather broad terms the principles by which the measurement team evaluates the impact of the Institute's programs. In the next section, we will describe in more detail several concrete examples of what the team's work looks like in practice.

Some Example Evaluation Studies

Because outcome measures are always context-dependent, the measures that the Institute uses for one-on-one coaching differ from those used to evaluate more narrowly focused competency training (for example, how to deliver feedback effectively, or how to delegate effectively). One of the primary complexities involved in measuring outcomes for one-on-one coaching is that, hypothetically, if you were to engage 100 students in one-on-one coaching, you could expect there to be easily 30 distinct goals that these students would be pursuing. (See Figure 7 from Chapter 4 for some examples.) This reality requires a multipronged approach to assessing the efficacy of professional coaching, as we can't possibly administer valid and reliable measures related to dozens of different goals before and after coaching. Although students do report at the end of the semester how much progress they feel they made toward whatever goals they were working on, an even more valid way to assess impact involves capturing changes in a standard set of outcomes that might reasonably be expected to change across most or all students involved in professional leadership coaching. Thus, in addition to asking students to report their subjective sense of goal progress at the end of the semester, the measurement team also administers a battery of scales to all students both before and after coaching to capture the following constructs:

- Leader identity (as described previously in this book)[118]
- Sense of purpose[119]
- Satisfaction with life[120]
- Psychological distress[121]
- Self-concept clarity[122]

In one study, the measurement team compared changes across all of these scales among students who were working with a leadership coach to similar changes among students taking an introductory psychology course who were not working with a coach (and had never done so previously). These non-coached students, who participated in the study in exchange for extra course credit, were randomly assigned at the start of the semester to one of two comparison groups. The first comparison group was given the same leader development plan that we give to students who are working with a coach, only they completed this plan online by themselves. Thus, this group thought about the concept of leadership, reflected on their personal values and their "leadership best self," and articulated one or more goals that they might want to pursue related to growing as leaders. But there was no follow-up and no accountability. There was no feedback or interaction with a trained professional to help them pursue their goals. We'll call this the "leadership self-reflection group." Other students were randomly assigned, instead, to a parallel condition in which we changed the language of the leader development plan to refer to time management rather than leadership. Like the leadership self-reflection group, these students completed the self-reflection exercise online and on their own. We will call this the "time management self-reflection group." Students in both of these comparison groups also completed all of the same measures that the students in the coaching condition completed (leader identity, sense of purpose, etc.), both at the beginning and the end of the semester. Throughout the semester, students in the coaching condition met with their leadership coach (virtually or in person) between three and five times for approximately an hour each time, completing their own leader development plans in conjunction with their coach.

Table 3, below, shows how these groups changed (or didn't change) over the course of the semester. For the sake of simplicity and because the leadership and time management self-reflection groups looked exactly the same across these outcome measures, we have combined the data from the two non-coaching groups in the table. It is also worth noting that the students in the coaching and non-coaching groups were statistically identical with respect to a wide range of demographic characteristics, with the exception of gender, but controlling for gender in our analyses did not have any effect on the results.* As Table 3 shows, students in the coached group exhibited statistically significant changes in four out of the five outcomes that were examined. The only outcome measure that didn't change significantly for the coached group was psychological distress, on which they started out at an unusually low level (which makes it very difficult to see any changes—it was hard for them to get any lower in distress than they were when the semester began). In contrast, the two non-coached

---

* This is a statistical operation common in social science research. For readers who are not familiar with what it means to control statistically for a variable, such as GPA, this operation allows researchers to mathematically adjust scores on an outcome variable (in this instance, ELE scores) to equate two or more groups of people with respect to a control variable or variables. As a result, the scores on the outcome variable reflect what we would expect to observe if the groups had started out being the same on the control variable(s). When we cannot randomly assign people to groups, measuring and controlling for extraneous variables in this manner is an important part of understanding differences between groups.

groups of students did not change significantly on any of the outcomes that were measured.[123]

Table 3. Changes in five outcomes across coached and non-coached student samples (end of semester levels minus start of semester levels)

	Identity	Purpose	Satisfaction	Distress	Clarity
Coached	0.87	0.38	0.40	-0.09	0.40
Non-Coached	-0.06	-0.03	-0.07	0.12	0.02

Note: Identity = leader identity; Purpose = sense of purpose/meaning in life; Satisfaction = overall life satisfaction; Distress = psychological distress; Clarity = self-concept clarity. Changes represent raw score differences that subtract levels at the end of the semester from levels at the beginning of the semester on each outcome.

In a follow-up[124] to this preliminary study, the measurement team took an unusual next step in its examination of the impact of professional leadership coaching for college students. Taking a representative sample of students and randomly assigning them to participate (or not) in leadership coaching would be impractical and probably would not work. In coaching, the client does almost all of the developmental work. Such work is challenging and requires a fair amount of intrinsic motivation, which means that assigning students to participate in an intensive, long-term coaching engagement is an effort doomed to failure. However, as a close alternative, it is possible to take a group of students who have indicated an interest in participating in coaching—thus, they all have the high levels of intrinsic motivation necessary to grow and change—and to randomly assign some of these students to receive a coach. The remaining students can then be waitlisted, which means that they receive a leadership coach in a subsequent semester.

This type of waitlist-controlled study design allows researchers to exert an unusual degree of control over the coaching experience, as the waitlisted students serve as an experimentally determined comparison group whose outcomes (measured at the start and end of the same semester in which other students were working with a coach) can be compared to those of coached students. The results of this experiment confirmed what the measurement team found in the previous study—that coaching had, indeed, *caused* the changes the team had observed in leader identity, self-concept clarity, and so forth. Specifically, the waitlisted group did not experience *any* significant changes in any of the outcomes we measured, whereas the coached group experienced significant changes across *all* outcome measures, this time including reductions in psychological distress.

Such changes are important and meaningful, but the data from these studies ultimately depend on what students self-report. Because students spend time outside of their busy schedules working with a coach, it's possible they might want to justify that costly time investment, and as a result of this self-justification motive, the changes we have been describing might be somewhat biased. As we noted previously, this is one of the reasons that the measurement team likes to use a wide range of measurement types when it evaluates the effectiveness of the Institute's initiatives.

To address this potential bias, the measurement team examined several sources for corroborating observational evidence. One of those corroborating sources is the professional coaches themselves. We previously reported data in Chapter 3 that showed how coaches' observations of student growth paralleled the changes in leader identity that came from students' own self-reports (despite the fact that the coaches had no access to students' self-report data at any time). In addition to observations from professional coaches, another source of corroborating evidence for student growth comes from a very different place: other students. One semester, the measurement team solicited students who were working with a leadership coach to nominate a peer who knew them well and had regular contact with them. The team then contacted these nominated acquaintances at the end of the semester and asked them to rate the amount of growth they had observed over the last few months in the coached student. The measurement team specifically asked these acquaintances for their growth observations regarding three, coaching-relevant domains: (1) self-awareness, (2) self-confidence, and (3) whatever specific goal the student in our coaching program had been working on with his or her coach. (These were obtained from the coached students themselves; examples of the most common goals were self-regulation, delegation, and empathy).

In a study design that exemplified the use of non-dependent variables, described earlier, the measurement team contrasted acquaintances' reports of observed growth across these three coaching-relevant domains with their reports of coached students' growth on three other, non-coaching-relevant domains: (1) concern for the environment, (2) enthusiasm for Rice athletics, and (3) interest in cultural diversity. These three dimensions were selected as non-dependent "foils" because they were relevant to college students on our campus, might be expected to change over time, and would be considered to be "socially desirable" characteristics within our sample. However, none of these three foils reflected a goal that students had ever chosen to work on with their leadership coach in any previous semester. For simplicity, we will report the average rating across these three foils to compare with the three coaching-relevant dimensions described above.

The graph below shows the results of this study, which includes data from 34 friends, roommates, and other acquaintances of students participating in the professional coaching program. Specifically, acquaintances reported observing significantly higher levels of growth on all three coaching-related dimensions compared to the coaching-irrelevant foils. Thus, these data provide a second source of corroborating evidence that the changes in leader identity and other outcomes we have described among coached students reflect *real* changes, changes that can be observed by other people who see them daily, who know them relatively well, and who have little to gain by exaggerating their observations of growth.

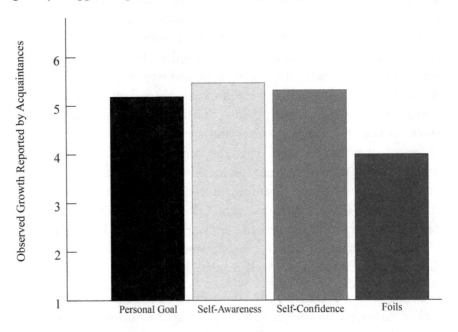

Figure 9. Observed growth reported by acquaintances of students who had worked with a leadership coach

The results we have described so far all pertain to the Institute's oldest and largest program to date, one-on-one professional coaching, and we already described in Chapter 2 how we use professional observers to evaluate students' coaching skills within the CoachRICE program. Assessments of the Institute's newer programs, while more preliminary, have likewise been encouraging and have yielded important insights into what has and has not worked in our attempts to help students grow as leaders.

For example, in addition to providing students with their own leadership coach, the Institute also offers students the opportunity to participate in group coaching with their peers in sessions organized around certain themes. Example themes include "Communicating with Confidence and Clarity" and "Overcoming Perfectionism." Although these themes are somewhat broad, they allow us to narrow down the types of outcomes needed to assess changes in students, in contrast to the more idiosyncratic outcomes in one-on-one coaching.

- **Communicating with confidence and clarity.** The measurement team used or adapted a variety of measures from standard, validated scales, which include assertiveness, social self-confidence, and rejection sensitivity.[125]
- **Overcoming perfectionism.** The measurement team adapted four validated measures from prior research for this training to cover a wide spectrum of outcomes associated with perfectionism and its consequences for leaders, including self-concept clarity, perfectionistic thoughts, perfectionistic feelings, and willingness to delegate.[126]

Likewise, Catalyst training modules involve two, two-hour sessions and are designed to develop specific leadership skills in students by giving them a mixture of relevant information and practice in the particular skill domain. These sessions occur two weeks apart to give students time to practice the skills they are learning between sessions, and the measurement team assesses changes in students two to four weeks post-training to determine how well the training "sticks."

- **Conflict management.** Students' strategies for managing conflict effectively are measured with a standard, well-validated scale that encompasses a wide range of conflict management approaches, including yielding, competing, avoiding, compromising, and problem solving.[127]

- **Delivering feedback.** This skill is fundamentally behavioral in nature. Thus, the measurement team assesses the impact of this Catalyst module with an observational rubric (created in-house) used by trained observers who are not involved in the intervention to evaluate students' skills in delivering feedback to others. As with other Catalyst modules, the measurement team examines the degree to which the training produces significant changes in students from before to after training.

Beyond "Smiley Sheets"

We opened this chapter noting that many of the universities that the Doerr Institute surveyed about their leader development programs stop short of true impact assessment by relying only on student satisfaction surveys to justify their program's existence. When we conduct impact assessment on our training programs, we go far beyond screening for mere satisfaction in an attempt to ensure that what we offer to students actually improves their ability to lead in a measurable way. That doesn't mean that so-called "smiley sheets" aren't important; after all, if students don't find that working with us is satisfying, they aren't likely to keep showing up or to encourage their friends to join them. It just means that satisfaction ratings alone don't represent the actual, ultimate outcomes that we really care about. Such ratings might be a beginning, but they must not be the end.

If the measurement team determines that there's not a meaningful difference in students as a result of training or coaching, that's when we have to make tough decisions about individual trainers or programs. As an example, one of our first Catalyst training modules for graduate students was highly rated by the students who participated in it. However, the measurement team was unable to find evidence that this training was helping students develop the targeted leadership competency. Even in cases like this in which students are clearly enjoying a training program, if it's not helping them become better leaders, then it's a waste of their time and the Institute's resources. When this occurs, the leader development team goes back to the drawing board and makes adjustments to the training. In many instances, this isn't as simple as just eliminating a program, since the topic of the training might be deemed to be critical for effective leaders. But to be effective, a program might need to be suspended while it is being redesigned and refined by the leader development team. In the case of the failed Catalyst module for graduate students referenced above, after the leader development team made some adjustments to the training's content and delivery, the measurement team tested the training again and found more encouraging results than had occurred in the pilot, with no loss in student satisfaction (if anything, satisfaction slightly increased after it was redesigned).

Sometimes when examining outcomes empirically, we discover things that lead to unexpected changes in our approach. As one example, early in the development of the Activation program, we assumed that freshmen were not ready to engage in professional leadership coaching. We did not make this decision based on evidence but rather on intuition and consensus, both among the Institute's full-time staff and our cadre of professional leadership coaches. This was a case in which we all agreed that it would be a waste of resources to allow freshmen into our Activation program, so they were arbitrarily excluded. After a few semesters, we decided to self-skeptically examine this assumption by actually coaching freshmen. What we found surprised us all and defied the proclamations of some of our most experienced coaches. Although freshmen might sometimes be more challenging to coach than older students, they exhibited changes in leader identity and other measured outcomes that were just as large, if not larger, than the changes exhibited by older students. Furthermore, when we examined the ratings made by our coaches of individual students, we saw that despite some of our coaches' protests that freshmen were not ready for coaching, the data told a very different story. Coaches rated freshmen as being just as highly engaged in the coaching process as they rated older students.

Thus, across multiple indicators, our intuitions were disconfirmed. This utter failure to intuit the truth was both humbling and exciting—humbling because we could not have been more wrong (or judgmental!) and exciting because it meant that we could begin working with students a full year earlier than we had previously believed possible. That fact meant that, as we rolled out additional opportunities to develop students as leaders, we could potentially see greater impact on their leadership abilities over time. As a result, our program grew faster and to a scale we could not have achieved without checking our assumptions with data.

Measuring Longer-Term Impact

So far in this chapter, we have focused our discussion of measured impacts to short-term outcomes—changes in leader identity or sense of purpose after a semester of professional coaching, changes in self-confidence or perfectionism after a semester of group coaching, and changes in narrower leadership skills, such as conflict management or the ability to deliver effective feedback, up to a month after training. But how long do such changes last? And if they are only short-lived, how much of a difference do our efforts make toward the longer-term goal of enhancing the ability of students to lead beyond their college years?

We have begun to investigate this question in several ways, one of which is currently the most objective, behavioral measures of impact that we have employed to date. We call this measure the *emergent leadership experience* (or ELE) score. To create this measure, we spent a year conducting focus groups and surveys of student leaders to help us code every leadership role on campus for the degree of leadership responsibility that each role entails, from treasurers of small student clubs (a role with a much lower level of leadership responsibility) to residence hall presidents[*] (a role with a high level of leadership responsibility). Although all such roles involve a degree of service to the school and sometimes the community beyond Rice, not every role demands the same level of leadership of other people. If we are truly having the transformational impact that we hope to have, then we would expect to see an increase in students' likelihood of stepping into formal leadership roles as a result of their engagement with the Institute (even though we don't equate leadership with formal titles or authority, nor do we press students to take on leadership roles that they are not currently pursuing). Likewise, if students who are involved in one-on-one coaching or other initiatives at our Institute are experiencing real, observable growth in their leadership abilities (as suggested by the preliminary results that we described previously), then it logically follows that these students would be more likely

---

[*] At Rice, undergraduate students are assigned to a residence hall when they matriculate, and these residence halls are actually called "colleges" (similar to the Oxford University model in the UK). Colleges at Rice are not only places to live; they also have unique identities and community governance systems, such that even alums of the university often continue to associate themselves with their residential college after they graduate. Because "college" usually means something else within the American university system, we use the more typical "residence hall" here for clarity.

to obtain the peer support needed to be able to step into leadership roles with higher levels of responsibility.

Using university-wide data from Rice's senior exit survey, we can calculate an ELE score for every graduating senior based on the levels of leadership responsibility entailed by all of the leadership roles they held as seniors, including within student-run businesses, student government, clubs and service organizations, and the residential colleges (in which the vast majority of all Rice undergraduates live). The ELE score, thus, provides us with a longer-term, behavioral index of the Doerr Institute's impact on students, without any of the self-reporting biases inherent to subjective evaluations.

One of the first things we discovered during this project was that just under half the student body was shouldering the majority of the leadership responsibilities on campus. That fact alone was interesting to us, as prior to this analysis, we didn't know what the distribution of leadership responsibilities would truly be. Furthermore, we found very few links between demographic variables and ELE scores, the two exceptions being gender and domestic (versus international) student status. To our surprise, women occupied leadership roles with slightly higher levels of responsibility, on average, than the roles occupied by men. Confirming anecdotal reports that international students held back from leadership roles while they attempted to acculturate and enhance their language skills, we also found that international students earned about a third of the average ELE score that domestic students did. Apart from these two demographic differences, no other meaningful differences emerged in our analyses across groups.

The question, then, was whether students who had worked with the Doerr Institute to develop their leadership abilities earned higher ELE scores than students who had not. Table 4, below, shows they did. Specifically, controlling for student's gender, international status, and cumulative GPA, we found that students who had worked with us before their senior year at Rice earned significantly higher ELE scores as seniors compared to students who had never worked with us. The former group was also significantly more likely to have earned *any* ELE points during their senior year compared to the latter group. These differences are particularly noteworthy given the fact that students who come to the Doerr Institute begin with slightly *weaker* leader identities than the rest of the student body (see Figure 4 back in Chapter 3), which includes their confidence and willingness to lead.

Table 4. Emergent leadership experience (ELE) scores as a function of whether or not students had worked with the Doerr Institute

	Average ELE Scores[a]	%Leading[b]	Sample Size
Doerr Students	2.28	57.1%	131
Non-Doerr Students	1.26	38.4%	742

[a] The difference between these averages was statistically significant in an analysis of covariance, $F(1, 868) = 21.8$, $p < .001$, controlling for differences among students in domestic (vs. international) status, gender, and cumulative GPA.
[b] The difference between these percentages in students earning at least one ELE point from the leadership roles they held was statistically significant in a logistic regression analysis, $B = 0.78$, $SE = 0.20$, Wald $= 15.77$, $p < .001$, odds ratio $= 2.19$.

In future analyses, we will be able to determine whether the timing of leader development interventions makes a difference in students' behavioral trajectories. Perhaps even more interesting, we will be able to evaluate the ways in which leader identity and formal leadership responsibilities influence one another over time. We suspect, as other leadership scholars have theorized,[128] that engaging in formal leadership enhances leader identity and that stronger leader identities motivate and enable people to step into leadership roles with greater levels of responsibility. In other words, their relationship is "reciprocal," or mutually reinforcing (or mutually *diminishing*, as might occur when people try and fail to lead well). Whether and to what extent such a reciprocal association occurs, and whether it occurs differently for different groups of people, will be possible to ascertain over time with access to the large samples of students we are able to track over their time in college.

Beyond the analysis of formal leadership responsibilities, we have recently begun to explore some of the secondary benefits of leader development. Although we have already identified some of the well-being benefits of working with a professional coach, these benefits could have their own subsequent consequences, both for students and for their institutions. For instance, students who experience growth in well-being might subsequently experience academic and social benefits. Institutions that have more students who are psychologically and socially healthy could experience lower costs associated with treating students for mental health needs, and they might even see increases in student retention and graduation. As these examples illustrate, the potential for downstream effects of the types of social interventions that we have initiated through the Doerr Institute are substantial.

Another example of returns on investments in leader development that we have examined concerns student employment and alumni engagement. If we are successful in enhancing students' leadership abilities, it would not be surprising to see some small benefits accruing to students when they enter the labor market. To evaluate this possibility, we recently examined employment-related data from the graduating class of 2019 as a function of whether or not students had engaged with the Doerr Institute specifically and whether they had participated in other leader development initiatives across campus. The latter question allowed us to start teasing apart the extent to which any associations we might observe between engagement with the Doerr Institute is simply a consequence of our attracting a certain kind of student—in other words, whether any association we might see between leader development through the Doerr Institute and employment-related outcomes is simply an instance of selection bias (an ever-present concern for people conducting program evaluation research). As we have already noted, very little appears to distinguish "Doerr students" from the rest of the student body at Rice, at least in terms of basic demographic factors (e.g., gender, race/ethnicity), academic factors (e.g., major, GPA), or psychological factors (e.g., extraversion, conscientiousness).

The source of the outcome data that we examined was the 2019 senior class exit survey, which students completed during the two weeks prior to graduating. The two primary student outcomes we examined from this survey were whether students had accepted a job offer at the time they completed the survey, and if so, what their starting salary was. For these employment-related analyses, we excluded students who indicated that they were pursuing graduate school rather than entering the job market, as well as students who were entering the military service or full-time volunteer service, such as through the Peace Corps. In addition to these two primary outcomes, we also examined a third outcome: how meaningful students rated the work that they were planning to do, for those who had accepted a job offer. This secondary outcome was included in our analyses in case engaging in leader development initiatives on campus somehow compelled students to seek less meaningful work by prioritizing the practical concerns of basic employment or the pursuit of material wealth over subjective purpose and meaning.

Table 5, below, shows the results of our analyses of employment and starting salaries for these graduating seniors. Our first finding was that students who had engaged in leader development work with the Doerr Institute were significantly more likely to have accepted a job at the time of the survey compared to students who had not. The difference between these groups was not only statistically significant (meaning, it was not mere statistical "noise" but was reliable and real); it was also quite large. The same was true for the average starting salaries of Doerr students and other students, which differed on average by about $10,000. For the almost 100 Doerr students in this study, that's a financial return of *almost $1 million to students*, a sum that we expect will only grow as we graduate more students who have engaged with us in developing their leadership abilities.

Futhermore, because we had access to data from a separate, campus-wide survey that asked students about their involvement in all leader development programs across the university (in addition to the Doerr Institute), we were able to measure how many such leadership initiatives each student had participated in during their time at Rice. Examples of these other initiatives include monthly "lunch and learn" workshops run by the Student Affairs office, a civic engagement program, and a peer advisory program. (We will return to the topic of these other leader development programs in the next chapter.) Controlling for student engagement in all of these leader development initiatives had almost no effect on the employment and salary results, even though we were missing data on a number of students for this selection bias analysis (which means that the sample size is reduced for these analyses—shown in Table 5, below, in the columns labeled "Adjusted").

Table 5. Percentage of graduating seniors who had accepted a full-time position with an employer at the time of senior exit survey and average starting salaries reported by employed students

	%Employed[a]	%Employed[b] (Adjusted)	Av. Salary[c]	Av. Salary[d] (Adjusted)
Doerr Students	76.3 (n = 135)	76.0 (n = 121)	$79,762 (n = 96)	$79,707 (n = 87)
Other Students	66.7 (n = 445)	66.4 (n = 405)	$69,975 (n = 283)	$69,301 (n = 254)

[a] Chi-square was statistically significant, $\chi^2 = 4.42, p < .05$. [b] Chi-square was statistically significant, $\chi^2 = 4.02, p < .05$.
[c] GLM-ANOVA was statistically significant, $F(1, 377) = 7.94, p = .005$. [d] GLM-ANCOVA was statistically significant, $F(1, 338) = 8.76, p = .003$.
Note. Sample sizes are indicated by "n." Respondents do not include students headed to graduate school, the military, or full-time volunteer service (e.g., Peace Corps). Levene's test for equality of variances (salary analyses) revealed that the groups did not differ significantly in their variances.

We were more than a little surprised by these results, to be perfectly honest. We knew that students experience meaningful change as a result of investing in their own leadership abilities. We had documented such changes semester after semester across outcomes such as leader identity, sense of purpose, and self-awareness. But the strength and robustness of these secondary outcomes were still surprising to us. Importantly, we found absolutely no reduction in how meaningful students felt the work was that they were entering into, as a function of whether they were Doerr students or not. Thus, we had not inadvertently fostered a shift in the prioritizing of materialism over meaning in students as a result of our leadership coaching or other programs.

In addition to these student-focused outcomes, the university also tracks a variety of outcomes related to alumni engagement, including whether or not students have (1) created their university-hosted online alumni networking account, (2) attended Rice alumni events, (3) volunteered to serve Rice in official capacities (e.g., conducting interviews of prospective students), and (4) donated to Rice. We have analyzed data from the 2017, 2018, and 2019 graduating cohorts across these four outcomes both individually and combined across outcomes, and the results we report below are remarkably robust to the method of scoring that we employ. Thus, for the sake of simplicity, we focus on just two metrics for these analyses: the *loyalty ratio*—the total number of alumni engagements across all four outcomes divided by the number of years since students graduated—and whether or not students have *donated to Rice*—one of the indices *within* the loyalty ratio.

Table 6 presents the results of our analyses of both the loyalty ratio and whether or not students donated to Rice at least once. As this table shows, engagement with the Doerr Institute significantly predicted both the broader loyalty ratio and the tendency to donate specifically. Adjusting these analyses for student engagement in other leader development programs across campus, which limits the data to seniors graduating in the spring of 2019 because of the availability of these additional data, has little effect on these outcomes. This suggests that the apparent "Doerr effect" on these alumni engagement outcomes is, once again, not just about the kind of students who seek to develop themselves as leaders.

Table 6. Alumni engagement levels across the broad metric of the loyalty ratio and the specific metric of whether or not alumni have donated to Rice

	Loyalty Ratio[a]	Loyalty Ratio[b] (Adjusted)	Dontating[c]	Donating[d] (Adjusted)
Doerr Alums	2.52 (n = 454)	3.45 (n = 202)	79.1% (n = 454)	81.6% (n = 202)
Other Alums	1.42 (n = 2229)	2.40 (n = 665)	63.2% (n = 2229)	67.1% (n = 665)

[a] General Linear Model ANOVA was significant, $F(1, 2681) = 223.34, p < .001$. [b] General Linear Model ANCOVA was significant, $F(1, 864) = 37.60, p < .001$. [c] Chi-square was significant, $\chi^2 = 42.2, p < .001$. [d] Chi-square was significant, $\chi^2 = 15.85, p < .001$.
Note. Sample sizes are indicated by "n." Loyalty ratio is calculated using the total number of indices on which alumni engaged across 2017–2019 divided by the number of years since graduating. Columns labeled "Adjusted" are statistically controlled for student engagement in other campus-wide leader development opportunities (data for this control variable are only available for a subset of students graduating in 2019, which is why the sample size for these Adjusted analyses is smaller).

Beyond these important benefits for students and the university, there are potential insights related more broadly to the practice of leader development that we are poised to discover by taking outcome measurement seriously. Our professional coaching enterprise, for instance, differs from the general practice of executive coaching, which tends to occur in small-scale engagements with solo practitioners or within a corporate environment in which confidentiality trumps openness as a priority. Our unique "laboratory" at Rice University and the fact that we are not selling anything to anyone position us to explore best practices in leadership coaching with sample sizes that facilitate robust, scientific conclusions about what works and what doesn't to help people grow and develop.

For instance, we could assign a randomly selected group of our coaches to receive certain types of advanced training related to goal setting; the identification of toxic, self-limiting beliefs; or the science of behavior change, and we can subsequently compare these coaches' effectiveness compared to other coaches who did not receive this training. (We've done this, by the way.) We can also modify some of the goal-setting and planning tools that we provide to students or broaden aspects of the coaching process itself (e.g., the number of sessions that students can have, the virtual vs. in-person medium) to see if such changes enhance the likelihood of students making progress toward their goals or experiencing bigger changes on the outcomes that we examine. With a valid and reliable set of outcome metrics in place and the will to apply basic research design principles to the process of behavior change, the possibilities abound. And we are willing to give away what we learn to other institutions that share our vision for helping students develop the leadership abilities that they need to make a difference in the world.

Conclusion

In this chapter, we have described a variety of examples of how the Doerr Institute takes a rigorous approach to measurement. The point of these examples is not that they are the be-all-end-all of outcome measures. They are just examples. However, we hope that they give readers a sense of what is possible when measurement of outcomes is taken seriously. It is possible to measure growth in specific elements of leadership, from identity to engagement in formal leadership roles. It is possible to evaluate the return on investment of leader development programs, both in the short term and the long term. Anyone who says differently might just be hiding something. Investing financially in the rigorous measurement of your leader development initiative takes a bit of courage, to be sure—after all, your own data might reveal that you aren't having the impact that you hoped to have on students. But in the end, we believe it's better to know this so you can change your approach than to continue in blissful (but impotent) ignorance.

In the next chapter, we will discuss our core operating principles, to which we have already alluded in previous chapters, in more detail. For those who are now convinced that it is time to "up their game" when it comes to developing students as leaders on their campus, Chapter 6 will help them establish a firm foundation for their efforts.

FOR REFLECTION: Do You Have the Right Metrics in Place to Examine the Effectiveness of Your Leader Development Program?

Many leader development programs fall victim to the common pitfalls of group-think, the confirmation bias, and the Good Samaritan bias. Prioritizing measurement to determine primary and secondary outcomes of leader development initiatives can help avoid these problems and demonstrate your ability to deliver on your promises to produce the next generation of leaders. Consider the following challenge questions related to your commitment to outcome measurement:

1. Do you measure all leader development initiatives in ways that fit the purpose and context of each initiative, rather than holding to only one type of measure or examining only one type of outcome?
2. Do you strive to minimize bias through objective research conducted by a professional who is not invested in the success of any particular program or initiative (in other words, someone who is not evaluating his or her own efforts)?
3. Do you measure changes in a variety of outcomes both before and after your training or intervention? Do you use reasonable comparison groups whenever possible (and random assignment to groups in the best cases)?
4. Do you draw upon existing research to determine the right measurement models and instruments for your programs and tune those findings iteratively with the content of the training?
5. What would you do if you discovered that one of your initiatives was not producing any measurable changes in students' ability to lead? Is your primary commitment more to the use of a particular method than to whatever methods produce the best results?

Chapter 6

ESTABLISHING FIRST PRINCIPLES:

How to Create the Conceptual Framework of a Leader Development Enterprise

In the Introduction, we identified some of the problems behind citizens of the United States' declining trust in its institutions and leaders. To recap, this is a challenging time for leaders globally; you don't have to look far to find examples of poor leadership and corruption. From pharmaceutical companies falsifying data on product efficacy to tech companies helmed by CEOs who are abusive to their employees to financial institutions that open accounts for clients without their permission, individuals and institutions are cultivating cynicism toward leadership. U.S. government leaders have abysmal approval ratings that *top out* in the 20th to 30th percentiles.

It seems pretty clear that the nation's leadership deficit can be traced back, in part, to a higher education system in which leader development is broken, as we described in Chapter 1. The absence of a leader development strategy leads to overeducated and underdeveloped leaders by the millions each year. This is a huge problem but not a hopeless one, as we have described evidence throughout this book that something *can* be done to address these challenges in relation to critical constructs, such as leader identity and specific leader competencies. With this evidence in mind, we'd now like to share a set of principles that have guided the Doerr Institute in its efforts to develop students as leaders. Once again, we do not suggest that our approach is the only way or even the best way to develop students' capacity to lead, nor are we arguing that the principles that we describe in this chapter are the only principles anyone should follow. But for institutions looking to take the first step in a concerted effort to make leader development a core feature of their missions, these principles can provide a path for creating their own, customized strategy for high-quality leader development.

The Doerr Institute's First Principles

In 2019, the Doerr Institute team met with a dedicated educator who sought our input as she began creating a leader development program at her college. Her first step in designing the program had been to contact the college's department heads and request that they each put forward the names of two students from within their departments as candidates for the new program. After selecting the students, the educator then hired an administrator to run the program. Although the administrator was undoubtedly well-intentioned, he had no professional leadership training, little input into how the program should be structured, and no say in the outreach to student participants. At the educator's request, we offered feedback, and suggested that she review the elements of her proposed program through the lens of the Doerr Institute's foundational elements—our First Principles. It is our belief that no matter what principles such programs adopt, unless they determine their own core principles as a starting point, these programs risk becoming like ships without a rudder.

We predict that over the next 10 years or so, all top-tier colleges and universities in the United States will be much more serious and systematic about leader development than they are today. For institutions that are ready to get serious now, we recommend starting by developing their own set of First Principles. If there is one category of college or university that comes closest to embodying our First Principles, it would be the national military academies. As discussed in Chapter 3, their public mission statements and culture all aggressively support leader development—not merely as a core function of their institutions but as their *most important* function.

These academies understand that one of the fundamental responsibilities of leadership is to give structure and definition to what an organization is, does, and stands for. Without that focus, success is more a fantasy than a goal. So if you've decided that it's meaningful to create a cutting-edge leadership development program, then it's well worth spending time at the front end constructing the foundation correctly. This understanding is what led us to establish our First Principles, which guide our mission to build a high-quality, scalable, leader development program serving the entire university.

Although the following list of principles doesn't cover every circumstance or decision that the Doerr Institute team encounters on a daily basis, these principles constitute the primary guardrails for us as we make decisions about what to do and what not to do. These principles are very broad, which means that there are many legitimate ways to apply them. So, although we would commend them to any college or university, we would never expect any school that adopted them to end up building a leader development program that looks just like ours:

1. Treat leader development as a core function of the institution.

Universities often refer to producing leaders in their mission statements. It makes sense, then, that they would assume that all of their students have potential as leaders and, correspondingly, would offer leader development opportunities to everyone they admit. However, most institutions also seem to single out only experienced leaders for development in small, boutique programs. Other programs with limited resources require students to compete for coveted slots to receive developmental opportunities. Because those who have grown up in privileged environments might tend to appear more "ready" than others for further development, both of these approaches result in students who have already been developed getting additional opportunities for more development. This means that those who *have* receive *more*, and those who *have not* receive *even less* (or perhaps nothing at all), which reinforces systemic inequalities that violate the principles of democracy and fairness.

We decided from the outset to reject these common approaches and, instead, allow students to decide for themselves when and if they are ready to be developed. Our experience is that only 30 to 40 percent of the student body will take advantage of leader development opportunities offered to them over the course of four years, and at this rate, our ability to develop everyone who *wants* to be developed can be managed successfully. When we conducted our research into leader development programs at universities across the country, which we described back in Chapter 1, it was always easy to identify when an institution did not have leadership as a core function of their mission. In our interviews with university staff and administrators, we would frequently hear assertions such as "we don't have enough money for that sort of thing." It's no secret, though, that universities find the money for their chosen, core functions. Many top-tier programs that "cry poor" about money for leader development actually have billions of dollars in endowments. They would never say no to programs that they have identified as being part of their core function, like physics or football. Once a university commits to treating leader development as central to its mission, then it's just a matter of translating that priority into a budgetary line item.

2. Use evidence-based methods to develop leaders.

As discussed earlier, universities are full of contrived activities that are labeled as leader development, including one-off workshops, retreats led by untrained staff or volunteers, speeches by famous (and expensive!) people, leadership yoga, and other "leader-tainment" events for students that are billed as leader development. Yet if you were to actually measure the outcomes of such initiatives, you would probably find that you have done little more than charm students; you didn't create leaders. Even courses on leadership taught by experts often do little to develop students' ability to lead. Whatever methods are chosen to develop students, what is most important is that they be evidence-based, with measured outcomes. No trust falls. No ropes courses. Why would anyone who is serious about the mission of developing students as leaders be willing to compromise for something less than industry standards and best practices?

When determining what an evidence-based method might be for developing leaders, we find it useful to draw a parallel to the level of evidence we would require of someone claiming that a medical treatment is evidence-based. A reasonable substitute for for a claim that an intervention is "evidence-based" is to say that it is "scientifically validated." The latter is helpful, insofar as it points us in the direction of common scientific practices for establishing an empirical claim as being supported or not supported by the facts. To claim that a leader development program or intervention is evidence-based, thus, means that someone with the training and qualifications to conduct scientific research on human beings has gathered actual data on the effects of that program or intervention, has done so in a manner that supports the validity of those data, has conducted appropriate statistical tests of those data, and has described the entire evidentiary process in an open and transparent manner subject to outside scrutiny by other trained researchers. In other words, a claim that a method for developing students as leaders must follow the scientific method. If it doesn't, then we should treat the claim as an empty promise. For a more detailed explication of this argument, as well as an explanation of relevant terms (e.g., reliability, validity, experimental versus quasi-experimental designs), we refer readers to Appendix 3.

3. Employ professional leader developers.

It stands to reason that people who are educated, trained, and experienced at something are better at it than people who are not. Universities wouldn't think of allowing amateur scientists to train graduate students in physics, but it's a different story with leader development enterprises. The norm that we have seen is for universities to routinely use well-meaning but untrained faculty mentors, staff, and volunteer alumni who want to give back to their alma maters but who lack the necessary expertise to make a meaningful difference in students' development.

The Doerr Institute only engages leadership coaches, trainers, and facilitators who have professional backgrounds and expertise. The use of untrained advisors, unqualified mentors, and uncertified coaches is an invitation for poor performance and unimpressive outcomes. (Anyone can call themselves a "coach," whether they have any professional credentials or not.) Individuals who don't meet such standards can often have great success at other educational and developmental programming. Mentors, for example, can be excellent for career development, but there are rarely standards for who gets to be a mentor, much less training for them before they begin. Additionally, their effectiveness is rarely, if ever, assessed, so in the end, they are likely to produce a lot of helpful conversations but probably not many long-term developmental changes in students.

A key reason why organizations often dip into the "amateur pool" for leader development is that the cost can be significantly less than the cost of hiring professionals. Beware of this false economy, because when you measure results, you see a clear difference between professionals and amateurs. What is the true economy of utilizing inexpensive leader developers if they don't successfully develop anyone? Recognizing the value of professionals should be a priority in constructing your leader development program. Similarly, we have found that *for roughly the equivalent of one full-time, senior faculty member offering classroom-based leadership training, we can individually coach 400 to 500 students*, an approach that we would argue is far more impactful in terms of producing leader development outcomes than more traditional, classroom-based lessons *about* leadership. This cost comparison makes the claim that using professionals for student leader development is "just too expensive" a hollow excuse.

Two ancillary concepts to keep in mind when selecting and training your leader developers include the following:

- Don't lump career training, networking, or other noble aims into the same category. People often confuse training (teaching corporate culture or policies) or career advancement (mentoring through networks, securing internships, or helping people advance in an industry) with leader development, which is solely focused on increasing the capacity or ability of an individual to lead. Although there can be real value in skill or career-focused training, conflating those with leadership allows institutions to check off the leader development box while potentially fooling themselves and also robbing their constituents of an opportunity to advance as leaders.

- Be wary of linking single demographic qualifiers to the term leader, such as "introvert leader," "engineering leader," or "female leader." Our own data show that women, international students, first-generation college students, and other historically underrepresented groups participate in and benefit from one-on-one coaching at the same levels as the overall student body. Although coaching certainly isn't the only way to develop leaders, it is the most individually tailored and inclusive method we know of to do so with reliable impact. So, although there might be a time and place to deal with single-demographic issues in leader development, the shortcoming of focusing on demographic issues is that when people lead, it's highly unlikely that they'll ever be in charge of a group isolated by personality, college major, or gender, much less race, ethnicity, sexual orientation, socioeconomic status, or any other single attribute. Likewise, the skills that leaders need don't demonstrably differ by any demographic characteristic, although they might be expressed to different degrees or in different ways across various groups of people and particular contexts. Programs aimed specifically at women and minorities are often popular, in part because of the growing recognition of the systematic, institutional barriers that have aggressively excluded such groups from leadership roles. However, from an institutional perspective, as a strategy for developing the most people at the lowest cost, such programs lack efficiency. Keep diversity training diversity training.

Related to our argument about the importance of using professional leader developers, it should go without saying that a leader development program ought to be headed by a professional with training and experience in leadership. Yet when we researched the leader development programs of more than 50 universities, none of the schools we examined had anyone in an authoritative role overseeing their leader development efforts across the university, such as a "Vice President for Leader Development" or a "Dean of Leader Development," much less a credentialed professional in the field. Instead, the schools we examined had small, boutique programs, usually operated several levels below a dean, and run by beloved, entertaining, and brilliant professors who had almost no actual experience at leading. People who are educated, trained, and experienced at something are better at it than people who are not. So choose your team carefully. To function effectively within an academic environment, the leader of your program will need to have some legitimate academic credentials in a related discipline, professional knowledge about leader development, and ideally, experience at leading organizations (so that the entire team will be well led). Knowing *about* leadership is not the same as being an effective leader, just as being an effective leader isn't the same as knowing how to develop others as leaders.

4. Measure outcomes ruthlessly.

Never let anyone tell you that leadership gains are intangible or impossible to measure. Those who say that developing leaders is more of an art than a science, or is something you can't possibly measure, are simply uninformed and incorrect, and we have described some of the evidence we have for this claim in Chapter 5. One of the reasons people might find it difficult to measure outcomes in this domain is that they are often attempting to measure the results of events that don't really produce many meaningful outcomes. In our experience, this is especially true of leadership classes, which are often examined using traditional course evaluations, rather than outcome measures of growth in leadership capacity.

Recently, a CEO of a top leadership development company expressed her belief to us that while business clients want to see measured outcomes, they don't care enough to pay for them, and this is why most business development and leadership organizations don't measure outcomes. A few months later, after being introduced to our First Principles, she contacted us again to tell us that she had decided to add an outcome measurement component to her leader development institute and *all* of her client work. Her experience echoes a trend for businesses increasingly to demand evidence of ROI for the work of coaches and other professionals in the leader development arena.

Similarly, our counterparts at another institution recently took some of the outcome evidence that we have gathered (and that we have described in this book—in particular, Figures 2 and 5) to decision-makers at their university, and they were able to garner $2 million in support of a pilot program to offer professional leadership coaching to their own students. Responding to this incredible success story, the vice president for student affairs at this university sent us the following note of thanks:

> We are so excited to develop the leadership capacity of our students. We cannot emphasize enough just how much the Doerr Institute enabled us to jumpstart this exciting new venture at [our university]. Your commitment to documentation and measurement made it easy for us to sell the idea to Student Affairs stakeholders. Your generosity and willingness to share your expertise is allowing us to accelerate our work and better serve our young [students]. We are so grateful to the Doerr team and your evolving work over the last few years. The Doerr methodology completely changes the student leadership development landscape.

A little evidence of impact can go a long way.

As we noted in Chapter 5, the Institute has an independent, full-time team led by an experienced social scientist with the sole responsibility of measuring outcomes objectively. This team is not tasked with trying to fix programs or design new ones; it simply has to determine if existing programs work or not. This allows us confidently to defund programs that don't produce measurable benefits and focus on those that do. Time and resources are too valuable to waste on programs that don't actually produce the benefits they were designed to produce.

For example, in the fall of 2018, we decided to assess the plethora of leader development programs offered at our own university. Our investigation examined how students' leader identities were associated with their participation in 10 campus-wide programs at Rice that claimed to develop students as leaders. These programs included the initiatives of large, well-respected centers (including, but not limited to, the Doerr Institute) to much smaller, less formal growth opportunities (such as becoming peer academic advisors and participating in "lunch and lead" seminars offered through the office of student affairs). We mentioned these other programs previously in this book, and we noted that students who had participated in one or more of the university's leader development opportunities exhibited stronger leader identities compared to students who had not participated in any of these programs (see Figure 4). But which of these programs were *independently* associated with stronger leader identity in students?

Using data from the university's campus-wide survey of student behaviors (on which we had included our standard measure of leader identity, as we've described previously), we were able to enter separately whether or not students had participated in each of these 10 leader development opportunities into a single, predictive regression model to examine whether participation in any of these opportunities was uniquely and significantly associated with student leader identity scores. In our model, which analyzed responses from over 2,700 Rice students, we also included student gender, international status, and level of leadership experience prior to coming to Rice (self-rated on a 5-point scale ranging from "none" to "an extreme amount") as control variables. What we found was that only two of these 10 programs predicted student leader identity. In fact, only participation with *one* other campus-wide program besides the Doerr Institute exhibited a significant, unique association with leader identity, such that students who had participated in this program exhibited stronger leader identities than students who had not.*

The robust failure across most of these programs and experiences is even worse than it might seem when you consider that, because all of these experiences were completely optional, many of them were likely to attract students who were already somewhat high in leader identity. Despite the likelihood of this kind of selection bias, most of these programs still failed to show a significant association with students' leader identities—meaning that the students who participated in these programs were no more likely to exhibit the confidence or the willingness to lead than were students who didn't participate in them. This is not an encouraging state of affairs. Still, perhaps we shouldn't be all that surprised about this result, considering that none of the other programs at our own institution appear to follow (or even articulate) the kind of First Principles that animate and guide the work of the Doerr Institute. If that sounds like a bold, even arrogant claim, perhaps it is. But the evidence appears to support it, no matter how bold it might seem, and it also is consistent with the findings we reported in the last chapter—specifically, that controlling for student engagement in other leader development opportunities on campus had virtually no impact on our ROI analyses of the Doerr Institute's work with students (e.g., Tables 5 and 6).

Our research into the leader development programs at other, top-tier universities across the country suggests that, for the most part, other insti-

---

* Specifically, the standardized regression coefficient for participation with the Doerr Institute was significant and positive, $\beta = 0.133$, $t = 7.52$, $p < .001$, as was the regression coefficient for participation in one other leader development opportunity, the Center for Civic Leadership, $\beta = 0.039$, $t = 2.17$, $p < .05$. These positive associations indicate that students who participated in either the Doerr Institute or the Center for Civic Leadership exhibited stronger leader identities than did students who participated in neither program. In a second analysis, we combined all of the non-Doerr Institute opportunities into a single variable, which could range from 0 to 9, and we entered this new variable into the regression model alongside participation with the Doerr Institute and our control variables (gender, international status, and prior leadership experience). In this new model, participation with the Doerr Institute was still significantly associated with leader identity, and participation in all other campuswide leader development opportunities was as well. However, the size of the association between leader identity and participation with the Doerr Institute was about twice the size of the association between leader identity and all other programs combined. Specifically, the standardized regression coefficient for participation with the Doerr Institute was significant and positive, $\beta = 0.134$, $t = 7.64$, $p < .001$, as was the regression coefficient for participation in all other leader development opportunities, $\beta = 0.067$, $t = 3.77$, $p < .001$.

tutions of higher education in the United States are unlikely to be doing much better than the individual programs at Rice. Most of the leader development at other schools we examined violated most or all of our First Principles. Consequently, year after year, American universities are graduating highly educated people who have not been effectively prepared to lead—quite literally producing college-educated people with high-school-level leadership skills.

Institutions considering what their own version of First Principles might look like should also consider how they will keep these principles alive over time. For our part, we hold a monthly, all-hands First Principles Lunch (yes, we actually call it that) to revisit and reinforce our principles. This friendly, open discussion allows the Doerr Institute staff to challenge its own thinking to ensure that it is staying on mission, identify where it might be deviating, and pinpoint what needs to change. This isn't the only way to keep people on-mission, of course, but without a strategy, it's easy to experience mission drift over time, only to wake up one day and find that you have become a leader-tainment shop rather than a leader development institute.

Shift Conventional Thinking with a Disruptive Viewpoint

No matter how strong your foundation or how solid your principles, without the courage to be contrarian in your approach, you will have a difficult time changing the status quo. But a small, committed minority can revolutionize beliefs and behavior and ultimately shift conventional thinking. A study published recently in *Science* reports the results from an experiment intended to determine the percentage of dissenters needed to reverse a majority-held viewpoint.[129] Significantly, the experiment was not about elite groups shifting majority opinion because of their outsized resources. Rather, what the study authors found was that social influence was more about "succeeding by being unrelenting." And the tipping point can be as low as just 25 percent. If the size of a dissenting group reaches 25 percent, a relentlessly committed minority can shift the entire group's thinking anywhere from 72 to 100 percent of the time, even when the majority had complete agreement prior to that point.

"One of the most interesting empirical, practical insights from these results is that at 24 percent—just below the threshold—you don't see very much effect," said Damon Centola, associate professor at the Annenberg

School for Communication at the University of Pennsylvania and author of *How Behavior Spreads: The Science of Complex Contagions.* "If you are those people trying to create change, it can be really disheartening." The difficulty, of course, is that it's often hard to gauge when you're near that 25 percent tipping point, so you can easily give up too soon.[130]

Since the inception of the Doerr Institute, we have considered 30 percent as the ideal percentage of Rice students to engage with its programs. Those 30 percentage points also dovetail nicely with the number of Rice undergraduates who "strongly agree" that developing their leadership abilities is a priority during their tenure at Rice. But, as study author Centola noted in referring to the 25 percent, "Approaching that tipping point is slow going, and you can see backsliding. But once you get over it, you'll see a really large-scale impact."[131] For us, that impact means shifting social norms at Rice, such that leader development becomes a greater priority within our community. We don't expect such a shift to convince *everyone* to devote large swaths of time working on their leadership skills. Some students simply are not ready to do so, and some might never wish to do so. But a shift in social norms might mean that those who *are* ready will decide to "go deep" with us and with others at Rice who offer students serious, professional opportunities to grow as leaders. When that happens, our students will be ready to become world changers.

FOR REFLECTION: Back to Basics

One of the fundamental responsibilities of leadership is to give structure and definition to what an organization is, does, and stands for. Without that focus, you have little chance of success. With this in mind, how would you answer these questions, derived from our First Principles?

1. Does your institution view the development of students as leaders to be at the center of its mission? What artifacts of your institution (e.g., mission statement, website, brochures) indicate that this is or is not the case?

2. Do you use evidence-based approaches to develop students as leaders? What is the nature of that evidence?

3. Do you employ professionals who are appropriately credentialed and trained to develop leaders, or are the people who run your programs mostly well-meaning but untrained individuals with an interest in students? Does your institution take

the same approach to hiring professional leader developers as it does to hiring faculty? In other words, does your institution hire faculty without advanced degrees or allow faculty to teach students in areas outside of faculty members' expertise?

4. Do you spend the time and resources to rigorously and carefully evaluate the results of your efforts to develop students as leaders? If not, why not? How do you know if you are succeeding in your efforts if you don't measure outcomes?

Chapter 7

AIMING HIGHER:

An Invitation to Professionalize Leader Development Together

At the end of her final coaching session, Divya, a kinesiology major at Rice, reached out to Ruth Reitmeier, the Institute's assistant director of coaching. Divya shared how pleased she was with her coach, Margaret, who had helped her navigate her university experience over the course of the semester:

> Over my sessions with Margaret, I have learned how to channel my perception of failure, success, and choices; how to approach goals systematically and realistically; and ways to take others' perspectives into consideration. Coaching with Margaret has been an incredible privilege, and she has helped me to be more confident, realize the extent of agency I have in my life and my actions, and has been an incredible support that has pushed me to pursue goals I would have previously been afraid to tackle.

Divya was reaching out not only to compliment her coach but also to request an additional coaching session with Margaret—one that would help her expand the leadership lessons she had absorbed at the Doerr Institute "beyond the hedges," which is a Rice expression for taking ideas and activities into the community beyond the border of hedges that surrounds the campus. Divya was in the midst of a project that had mushroomed into something unexpected, and her next step involved reaching out to a major company—Adidas. Margaret's coaching had played a large role in getting her to this point, so Divya understandably wanted to retain her coach's expertise to guide her through her upcoming contact with the mega-corporation.

Over the course of the semester when she was working with Margaret,

Divya began applying her newfound skills toward a global challenge she had identified. Specifically, in conjunction with her participation on the Rice track and cross country teams, she began volunteering at a nonprofit organization called ROMP—the Range of Motion Project—that delivers prosthetics to underserved populations in the United States, Guatemala, and Ecuador. After going to Guatemala with ROMP as a volunteer to deliver prosthetics to hospitals, she felt impassioned by the organization's mission and wanted to continue this meaningful work. During her travels, Divya learned of an app called atlasGO, which features digital campaigns that help raise funds and awareness for important issues by linking runners who want to make a difference with nonprofits and corporations to accelerate change.

In a moment of inspiration, she came up with the idea of having her entire track team log their total miles through the app and donate the miles to fundraise for ROMP. Divya jumped through the appropriate hoops to seek approval from the governing athletic association's director of compliance services for her idea, and she received clearance that all practicing competition miles that her team ran could be logged through the app. Once the challenge was completed and the money pledged was gathered, though, she didn't feel her job was done: "I was like, 'What are we going to do now?' I could have waited and let ROMP do their thing and start another challenge, but who knows how long that would have taken?" Instead of waiting for something to happen, Divya stepped up as a leader with an even bigger idea that would combine harnessing the power of her athletic teammates with corporate sponsorships to help fund ROMP's worthy cause. She thought, "Why not ask Adidas, which sponsors all of Rice athletics, to get on board and lend their corporate weight to the initiative?" And that's exactly what she did, step by step, until it culminated in writing a proposal letter to Adidas with the help of her Doerr Institute coach during the extra coaching meeting she requested and received. Divya had done the math and recognized that if her idea flew, with a corporate donation of $1 per mile, the women's cross country team alone could raise $15,000 for ROMP in just three months.

> I'm just seeing this as an untapped oil field right now for nonprofits to connect with [athletic] programs across the country and be sponsored by huge organizations like Adidas, or Nike, or New Balance, or Under Armor....It's a way for them to get connected with the prosthetics organization, which is an entire population of

people who are not served by these companies yet but still deserve to move.

Divya sees applications that could extend far beyond what she has already started to create for Rice, Adidas, atlasGO, and ROMP's underserved populations, since many nonprofits use the app's platform as a way to generate revenue. "There are so many ways that this could go, and I'm trying to start it really small and make sure that it works so that Adidas is encouraged and more interested to do bigger things later." She points to the guidance she received from being coached at the Doerr Institute for helping her expand her thinking about leadership beyond the hedges while also leading at Rice and putting the school in the headlines for being the first team in its conference to donate all of their miles to a nonprofit. "It just helps to have someone talk you through your ideas and get you to dig up what it is that you want to do and say," explained Divya. "And that's what Margaret did for me. She helped me realize that I have it all within me. I don't know if I would have done this had I not gone through the confidence building with Margaret...about approaching authority."

Divya's story is one of many examples of how Rice students leverage their newfound leadership skills to help change the world off campus and stretch outside of the university sphere into other arenas—in some cases, like hers, even before graduation. Likewise, in applying leadership lessons from the Doerr Institute long before donning a cap and gown, Carlos, the Rice engineering student whose story has been woven throughout this book, is another example of the hedge-jumping entrepreneurial mindset. After experiencing a taste of what it was like to develop leadership skills through the Doerr Institute in an area he cared deeply about—establishing his own start-up—Carlos found himself so interested in jumpstarting his leadership journey and making new connections *outside* of campus that he began attending engineering conferences around the country while still juggling his student workload.

"My end goal is the start-up world," Carlos explained. "At conferences, it's 100 percent networking. I'm using specifically what the Doerr Institute taught me to leverage those connections." Carlos also used skills that he learned at the Institute to connect with other Houston-based entrepreneurs during his travels, which widened his web of contacts in relation to his start-up. "I went on LinkedIn, looked up every single Rice grad that was in the Silicon Valley, messaged every single one, and had a breakfast, lunch, and dinner meeting with a different Rice alum every single day I was there." As a student who is concurrently running his own start-up (providing advertising on taxicabs in Mexico) that is in the process of expanding and hiring for the first time, Carlos has big plans for his business. "As soon as I'm out of school, that's what I'm focusing on," said Carlos.

> Being a leader is extremely important to me outside of Rice....I hope to implement these leadership techniques to promote the longevity of my company and of all future projects I work on by creating a culture around guidance and independence through leadership....I also hope to be able to train the employees I hire in my start-up to be better leaders both within the organization and in the communities we're working in to advance social change at a greater scale in whatever market we enter.

Darius, a former engineer at a large oil and gas company, sought out a coach while pursuing his MBA at Rice. A natural collaborator, Darius liked interacting with people in both his personal and professional life, but he tended to back away when difficulties arose. He said it was like a light bulb clicking on when he realized that he needed to deal with his own feelings, stay in the middle of the conflict, and learn to navigate through it, no matter how uncomfortable it made him. He believes that learning to assert himself and speak his mind dramatically improved his ability to lead a team. Now out of school and working as a consultant in Manhattan, Darius has abundant opportunities to flex his new skills. He knows how to give guidance to others, and he can handle the tough conversations, including the pushback he sometimes receives. By learning to say "I hear you, but I disagree and here's why," he feels he has stepped up to a new level of competence, which he credits to his coaching at the Institute.

A Vision for Transformation

In this book, we have argued that institutions of higher education in the United States, with only a few exceptions, are not living up to their own hype when it comes to the strategic, intentional, and systematic development of students as leaders. Many colleges and universities claim to do exactly that, but when pressed to articulate *how* they are doing so—as we have pressed a noteworthy sample of them to do—the answers are at best underwhelming:

- "A class on leadership is being taught over in the business school. It's very popular with the MBA students. At least 50 students each year enroll."
- "I'm not entirely sure what all we are doing. I think we have a lunch series over in the student union. I hear good things about it."
- "You'll have to ask someone else. I know we do a lot of things, but I couldn't exactly tell you what they are right now."

These are the types of responses we received over and over from representatives of some of the best schools in the country—schools we selected because someone, somewhere, had ranked them highly for their ability to develop students as leaders or because they themselves claimed to be the best at doing so. How can they be great at developing students as leaders when someone searching diligently for evidence showing the value of their approach is hard-pressed to find any such evidence at all?

When evaluating an empirical claim in science, we usually begin by assessing the claimant's theoretical framework first. Does the claimant have a reasonable theoretical basis for his or her predictions, or is it more like a loose set of speculations and ungrounded assertions? The theoretical framework that we have argued for in this book, when it comes to developing students' capacity to lead, begins with the integration of a strong leader identity and the social-emotional abilities often referred to as "emotional intelligence." Leader identity, in our framework, is defined by students' tendencies to categorize themselves as leaders, to feel confident in their ability to lead, to be self-aware of their strengths and weaknesses as leaders, and to be willing to lead when the opportunity arises, among other such qualities. People who don't think of themselves as leaders, who are riddled with self-doubt, or who lack even the desire to lead are unlikely to take on the burden of responsibility that leadership entails when the chance to lead presents itself, much less seek out such opportunities on their own. Thus, having a strong leader identity is fundamental to growing as a leader. Likewise, the suite of characteristics that typically fall under the heading of emotional intelligence are critical to leading effectively (and to being selected for leadership roles in the first place, as research on "leader emergence" has shown[132]).

Together, leader identity and basic, social-emotional skills make up the left and right posts of a ladder, the rungs of which are leadership competencies. To lead well, people need a host of concrete skills that past research has identified, such as the ability to manage conflict, to provide constructive feedback, to listen well (and to be open to what one hears), to adapt to changing situations, to cast a compelling vision that motivates followers, and a host of other such skills.[133] These are skills, furthermore, that can be trained, and a multi-billion dollar industry has sprung up outside of higher education to do just that. This industry does not always measure the extent to which it is succeeding in its training objectives, but when it does, the evidence to date indicates that investing in training for leaders can be money well spent.[134]

Of course, to know whether any training initiative is, in fact, achieving what it is designed to do requires that training objectives be defined, operationalized, and assessed empirically, and this is no less true of leader development efforts in higher education. Although empirical assessment of outcomes is increasingly common (though certainly not ubiquitous) in industry, it is almost completely lacking in higher education, as far as we can tell. There are exceptions, of course—for instance, one-off classes taught by leadership scholars who understand the scientific method and value the insights it can yield to help them achieve their goals—but these exceptions prove the rule. The irony of this pattern is difficult to ignore. The very universities where knowledge is created daily, leading to astounding breakthroughs in biology, physics, and chemistry, seem to forget how science is done when it comes to testing the hypothesis that they are truly developing students as leaders. Paraphrasing an early pioneer in the field of experimental psychology, if something exists, it exists in a measureable quantity.[135] If colleges and universities are, in fact, advancing the capacity of their students to lead, as they typically assert that they are doing, then the extent to which they are doing so ought to be measureable. If it's not, then perhaps we should question the assertion itself, rather than questioning whether such outcomes can be measured. They can be. We have done so, as have many others in the field of leadership research. The question isn't *can* we measure such outcomes but *will* we? And are we willing to believe and act on the results when we do?

We've provided a variety of examples to illustrate our own approach to measuring outcomes. We've described, for instance, how leader identity barely moves an inch from freshman to senior year for students who don't get involved in any of the possible leader development opportunities on campus, and how it *does* increase (a little) among students who do engage with one or more of these opportunities. After a semester with a professional leader development coach, leader identity improves substantially—a change that is driven, in part, by increases in the clarity of students' self-concepts. Students tell us that they make substantial progress toward their goals through professional coaching, and this assertion is supported both by what their coaches tell us and by what their friends and acquaintances report observing. We've also described some of the secondary, well-being benefits of professional coaching, as well as the longer-term associations between formal leadership responsibilities and involvement with the Doerr Institute.

The examples we have given in this book are only a sample of the kinds of impact data that we have gathered, of course. Each Catalyst training module has its own, specific objectives, and we measure the success of each and every one of these as well. One finding that we have not reported so far is a very simple one, but we feel it is worth mentioning here. It might even be one of the most important outcomes that we have observed to date, despite being deceptively simple. Each semester, as part of a modest advertising campaign for the Institute, we have a small cadre of student affiliates sit at a table outside of the Rice Coffee House at the student center. These affiliates hand out descriptions of our programs to interested students, and in return for completing a very short survey, passersby can get a coupon for a free coffee or treat. We use this survey as an opportunity to gather a little data on the student body, in part to ascertain how, if at all, students who (1) have worked with us in the past, (2) are working with us at present, or (3) think they might work with us in the future might differ from (4) students who tell us they have no interest in ever darkening our door. On the survey one fall semester, we asked students whether they were working on any personal development goals related to leadership and, separately, any personal development goals unrelated to leadership. We thought that perhaps being more goal-oriented was a way that students who invest time with us might differ from the uninterested. What we found surprised and intrigued us.

With respect to personal development goals that were *not* related to leadership, the four groups described above did not differ statistically. On average, about 60 percent of the student body said that they were presently working on a non-leadership goal and provided a detailed enough description of this goal that we could categorize it adequately. A few students, for instance, said they were working on a goal that wasn't really a personal development goal, such as wanting to one day go to law school, which—though a laudable desire—was not what we meant by this question. After we removed the small number of inappropriate responses, the four groups all showed roughly the same levels of goal pursuit. However, when we looked at the results of the leadership-related goals, the four groups were no longer the same. The table below shows these results. Bear in mind, as you examine this table, that the sample sizes within each group (labeled "N" in the table) almost perfectly matched the representation of these four groups on campus at the time that we gathered these data, so we suspected that the students in this survey sample did a reasonably good job reflecting a representative cross-section of the student body at Rice.

Table 7. The percentage of students in four groups who reported they were currently working on a leadership-related, personal development goal

	Non-Doerr/Closed	Non-Doerr/Open	Current	Past Doerr
	22%	29%	25%	41%
N:	41	173	16	90

Note: Non-Doerr/Closed = students who had never worked with the Doerr Institute and expressed no desire to do so; Non-Doerr/Open = students who had never worked with the Doerr Institute and expressed an openness to doing so in the future; Current Doerr = students who had recently signed up to work with a professional coach through the Doerr Institute but had not yet begun; Past Doerr = students who had previously worked with a coach through the Doerr Institute. N = sample size.

As this table shows, students who had never worked with us but were open to the possibility were very similar to students who had no desire to do so. Roughly the same percentage of students in both of these non-Doerr groups was working on a personal development goal related to leadership (e.g., being more assertive, communicating a vision for their teams) at the time of the survey. In contrast, students who had worked with a Doerr Institute leadership coach in the past were substantially more likely to be working on their own on a personal development goal related to leadership.[*] This difference was consistent with our suspicion that students who come to work with us are more goal-oriented than the rest of the student body at Rice, although they didn't appear to be more goal-oriented in

---

[*] A chi-square analysis on these frequencies revealed that the "Past Doerr" group was significantly different from all other groups combined, $p < .025$.

general—only with respect to leadership goals.

However, one group upended this interpretation. That group was the smallest by far of the four groups: students who had recently signed up to work with us (primarily through our coaching program). These students had not yet begun one-on-one coaching, importantly, but they *had* self-selected to be coached soon. This fourth group looked almost identical to the two student groups that had never worked with us before. That suggested students who self-select to become "Doerr students" were not different from the rest of the student body with respect to goal orientation—whether leadership or otherwise. Rather, students became more likely to work on a leadership-related goal on their own because they had previously worked with a professional coach. This was unexpected and exciting. It suggested, tentatively, that working with a leadership coach might have given students a model for goal setting that they carried forward with them long after their coaching engagements had ended or, at the very least, had bolstered their sense of self-efficacy so that they felt motivated and able to continue their growth. Either way, they were working on themselves without a coach's help. They were taking ownership of their development as leaders.

Despite our excitement at this finding, the critical group—students who had self-selected to be coached but who had not yet begun coaching—was too small for us to be confident of the right interpretation of these results. So we decided to ask students who signed up to get a professional leadership coach the same personal development questions we had asked about in our Coffee House sample. Despite the fact that this second sample was surveyed in January, the month that many Americans have a tendency to start the new year with a focus on initiating personal goals, students who had signed up to work with a professional coach but had not yet begun meeting with him or her were not especially likely to already be working on a leadership-related goal (only 31 percent were, in fact, similar to the Non-Doerr/Open students from the Coffee House sample).

Encouraged by this finding, we added the same question to a survey that we sent to a sample of Rice alumni later that spring. This sample was composed of 75 students who had worked with us as undergraduates at Rice and 103 students who had not and were matched with the Doerr student group on gender, race/ethnicity, and major (the two groups were incidentally identical on their cumulative GPAs at graduation, we should add). We thought it was possible that the "fluke" in our original sample from the Coffee House was not in the *small* group of self-selected but as-yet uncoached students after all. Instead, perhaps the fluke (if there was one) was in the *larger* group of students who *had* previously worked with a coach. Maybe the leadership self-development rate of 41 percent was the anomaly in the data set, a consequence of random sampling error. But even if it weren't an anomaly due to sampling error—if it were a true, replicable consequence of our coaching program—how long would this difference last? Would "Doerr alums" continue to exhibit an elevated rate of autonomous self-development a year or more after they had graduated from Rice?

They would, it turns out. More specifically, 44 percent of the 75 Doerr Institute alums reported that, at the time of the survey, they were working on a leadership-related goal that was not mandated by a boss or supervisor. In other words, no one was making them work on this goal or rewarding them for doing so. Their ownership over their own development as leaders continued to be elevated relative to their peers, among whom only 26 percent of 103 students were working on a personal development goal related to leadership, which is consistent with what we saw in our Coffee House data.

This small, seemingly inconsequential difference indicates a trajectory shift for students who work with us. A trajectory shift means that we aren't just giving students a "bump" in their ability to lead by the time they graduate, although a bump might be meaningful and potentially important. Rather, we are helping to alter the direction of their lives by equipping them to change themselves. Now *that's* the kind of change we can get excited about. That type of change is truly transformative.

Public Purpose Drives Leader Development in Higher Education

Throughout this book, we have encouraged a leadership reckoning, a call to more robust leader development offerings and measurement of outcomes in schools across the nation, particularly those claiming that they create leaders. However, we've also noted there are a few, select schools other than Rice that appear to have robust, strategic initiatives to develop their students as leaders. As we consider how to transform higher education to better live up to its promises of leadership development, it is wise to consider and learn from the promising practices of other institutions.

Specifically, sophisticated leader development strategies can be found throughout the nation's military academies.

Military academies stand out in the landscape of higher education for their treatment of leader development as a core function of the institution. As one example, the United States Military Academy at West Point, New York, has a longstanding commitment to cultivating leadership abilities in their graduates. Indeed, all of the national service academies go a step beyond in supporting leader development as a central component of their educational missions; their public mission statements and culture all aggressively support leader development as the most important function of their institutions. Their focus on leadership matches the culture of the profession of arms that their graduates will help to lead as officers in the armed forces.

West Point's approach to developing leaders emphasizes four domains: character, academic excellence, military leadership, and physical development. Each domain has carefully outlined criteria that cadets follow for the express purpose of achieving leadership excellence. West Point painstakingly articulates their strategic plan for institutional leader development in the West Point Leader Development System (WPLDS), a 47-month commitment that the organization describes as "purposeful integration of individual leader development and leadership development experiences within a culture of character growth."[136] Their vision, stated on the second page: "West Point is the preeminent leader development institution in the world."

This intense focus on leader development at West Point and the other service academies emerged in the late 1990s as the result of research from within their own behavioral science departments. These projects led the national service academies to embrace the idea that leader development, rather than attrition, was the best way to form and graduate strong leaders. One of the authors of this book (T. Kolditz) experienced much of this shift when serving as the department chair for Behavioral Sciences and Leadership at West Point from 2000 to 2012. Using this new approach, which drew on the developmental theories of academics like Robert Kegan[137] and Robert Sternberg,[138] the service academies lowered their attrition rates across the board from more than 40 percent to less than 15 percent while, at the same time, embracing evidence-based theories and methods of development. The significance of this shift to other universities is that the service academies demonstrated, for very practical reasons, that leader development can be made a core function of a university.

The shift was not a superficial touch up. The national service academies have additionally gone to extraordinary lengths to provide highly trained leader development staff for their cadets. Traditionally, cadets and midshipmen have been coached and developed by successful mid-career officers. But it wasn't until the late 1990s, in conjunction with the increased focus on leader development, that the U.S. Military Academy began sending their supervisory staff officers (approximately 25 per year) through a full-year master's degree in counseling psychology proffered by Long Island University, with the goal of giving these officers professional skills and a deep understanding of human development to support their military training and career growth. In 2005, the program was upgraded to an academic degree in organizational psychology and leader development from Columbia Teachers' College. The Naval Academy followed suit by offering a degree program at the University of Maryland, and the Air Force Academy created a similar program at the University of Colorado-Colorado Springs. This approach signals a significant payoff to using highly trained leader development staff, versus in-place professors or untrained mentors.[139]

Let's draw a comparison now to other schools. Across the military academies, as a rough estimate, one would find a highly trained leader developer for every 50 or so students—a massive investment, given that these selected leadership trainees are by necessity removed from the military personnel pool for a year of graduate school and (usually) then stay at the academy for three more years to develop students as leaders. To put that in perspective and equate it to other universities, at a large state school like the University of Illinois at Urbana-Champaign, an equivalent investment would require using 880 trained and experienced leader development professionals in daily development and coaching of students.

It is easy to make the mistake of looking at service academies and allowing the shiny brass buttons on grey wool to obscure the fact that, conceptually, their practices can be effectively replicated in many other colleges and universities. Just because the organizational structures in the military establish clear hierarchies does not mean that the leadership model is all "command and control." To the contrary, the cadets and midshipmen in these academies are taught the same influence principles that work well when leading in the private and public sectors. There is nothing uniquely military about intentional, professional leader development.

Broadening the Scope

An institutional commitment to leader development, however, goes far beyond military service academies. For example, entire reviews have been written about leadership training in schools of agriculture, of which there are more than 130 colleges and universities in the U.S. alone.[140] Schools with an expansive, diverse curriculum like Texas A&M strongly promote leadership development, including A&M's famous Corps of Cadets, where leader development is a prinicipal feature of the experience—not all students in the Corps will seek commissions and military service, but all are expected to develop as leaders. Beyond agriculture and military schools, Creighton University in Nebraska, and Fort Hayes State University in Kansas have both academic leadership curricula and strong leader development initiatives for large numbers of students. Seton Hall University's Buccino Leadership Institute delivers professional leader development across all the schools in the university. The University of Colorado at Boulder similarly launched an institution-wide Center for Leadership as part of their strategy to develop students as leaders across all their schools. These programs highlight the irony of college ranking systems. If you look closely at the highest ranked schools in the country, you will see leader development programs only for small numbers of elite or hand-picked students—no coherent, institution-wide strategies for developing students as leaders are apparent.

Leader development excellence in colleges and universities is independent of other achievements in teaching or research. Our intent is to help other institutions—large and small, well endowed or pay as you go—to figure out what it might mean *for them* to achieve excellence in this critical domain. We have no expectation that what others do will look like what we are doing at Rice. Even if other institutions adopted something close to our First Principles, these are simply principles. The way people put them into practice will look different from one institution to the next. And that's a good thing, in our opinion. If institutions that have a similar vision for professionalized leader development were to share their own experiments—both successes and failures—with others, we could all learn from one another. Indeed, we expect to continue to grow and modify our own approach as we learn more about what works and what doesn't. Continual innovation will be a requirement to succeed in this realm, as culture changes, technology changes, and people's needs change. Our ability to adapt to such inevitable instability would be substantially enhanced by having partners in this great endeavor—institutions with the same vision that are willing to be collaborative and transparent. In the short term, it is students who will benefit the most from our shared commitment to this mission, but through them, our society and the world at large will reap a harvest of rewards in the end.

To that end, we are partnering with the Carnegie Foundation for the Advancement of Teaching to create a way for colleges and universities to quickly self-examine the current state of leadership education and development across their institutions. Carnegie currently classifies colleges and universities in the U.S., Canada, and Australia in terms of their structure and activities. For example, strong research schools are classified as R-1 or R-2, whereas other schools are classified as Community Colleges or Doctoral/Professional schools. In addition to this somewhat routine classification, Carnegie has established elective classifications in areas where some schools are particularly adept, such as their Community Engagement elective classification. Carnegie plans to field a new elective classification, Leadership for Public Purpose, in the spring of 2021. The purpose of the classification is to recognize colleges and universities that have comprehensive, evolving, and effective practices around leadership education, development, and research. The real value of the classification is that the application requires a comprehensive self-examination, based on improvement science, and is intended to guide schools in the direction of teaching and training more and better leaders among faculty, staff, and students. Appendix 4 describes the classification application and serves as a blueprint for anyone who wishes to aggregate the leadership-related characteristics of their institution or organization.

A Challenge and An Invitation

It bears repeating that there is greater need than ever for effective leaders in our world. Our own democracy's future depends on morally fit and ethically trustworthy leadership. Every type of organization, business, industry, and social justice movement requires principled guidance and empathetic leaders. This type of leadership is a resource that can only be renewed when people choose to develop their leadership skills.

Our work to date has given us a glimpse into the future of leader development in this country. What we see is the importance of providing professional-quality leader development to college-age leaders early on in their careers—not waiting until they become identified as "high-potential" executives much farther down the road, when it's too late for optimum learning and maximum impact. As we've argued in this book, personalized and direct development in the university environment might change the trajectory of an individual for 50 years or longer. Early intervention with young leaders will reap dividends not only for the leaders themselves but also for the countless colleagues, direct reports, and organizations that they will work with over the course of their lifetimes.[141]

The field of higher education is experiencing a period of deep disruption, largely due to the combination of rapidly escalating costs (typical of industries whose expenses are driven heavily by human labor) and the opportunities afforded by changing technology. The rise of massive open online courses (MOOCs) threatens to upend the way that post-secondary education is delivered, but how that will ultimately change the broader landscape of colleges and universities remains unclear. Thirty years from now, will there be any traditional universities left in the United States, where students spend four or five years living in dorm rooms, going to frat parties, and gathering in musty-smelling classrooms to learn from a live professor standing in front of a chalk board? How will growth in artificial intelligence and virtual communication alter this traditional approach, which has stood the test of time for hundreds of years?

No one knows for sure. But as colleges and universities struggle to make the case that their traditional model of higher education is worth the lofty price tag, we find it strange that they wouldn't take seriously the opportunity to make professional-quality leader development part of their value proposition. How many better ways are there to make the case that attending an elite, traditional university is worth the cost? But schools will only be able to make this case legitimately if they interrupt the status quo and get serious about developing students as leaders. The traditional way of doing things will not stand up to close inspection. We will do all that we can to make sure of that. As more and more schools adopt professional approaches to leader development, such as the ones we have described in this book, those that refuse to let go of how they have always operated will find themselves left behind.

It doesn't have to be that way, though. Change is possible. It has been our privilege over the last few years to be able to share what we are doing with a large and diverse set of institutions. From the Air Force Academy to Seton Hall to the University of Texas, our emphasis on evidence-based practices, wielded by trained professionals and combined with rigorous measurement, is yielding results that are getting attention. While such attention is flattering, our vision is to promote a fundamental shift in how leaders are developed across the entire landscape of higher education. Rice University's own mission statement includes the desire to "cultivate a diverse community of learning and discovery that produces leaders across the spectrum of human endeavor."[142] This sentiment, as we have already noted, is echoed in the mission statements of many top colleges and universities. Our goal is to help colleges and universities to transition from lofty-yet-hollow statements about developing leaders to actually developing leaders in evidence-based, professionally executed ways, the outcomes of which are objectively measured—standards to which we hold ourselves accountable at Rice every single day.

A leadership reckoning is not a concluding event or an end in itself. It's an accounting of where things stand presently, but not a final judgment. It's the beginning of what may prove to be one of the most impactful changes in colleges and universities in this century. Let's learn from each other and animate this movement together.

Appendices

Appendix 1: The Doerr Institute Leader Development Plan

Student Name, Year, College, and Major(s):

Coach Name:

Getting to Know You

Provide brief responses to the following:

1. What is unique about you? What special knowledge, talents, traits, background, or abilities do you have?
2. What are you passionate about? What inspires you?
3. What would you do if you knew you couldn't fail? What do you think holds you back?
4. How do you spend most of your time and energy outside of class at Rice?
5. What do you like best about your life as a student at Rice? Least?
6. Anything else you'd like your coach to know about you?

Co-Creating Your Leader Development Plan

This Leader Development Plan (LDP) provides a way to structure and focus your leadership goals and activities as you work with your coach. **Please complete Part 1 of this plan before your first meeting with your coach. In your initial meetings, you and your coach can discuss Part 1 and co-create Parts 2 and 3.**

Part 1

Pre-Coaching Assessment: Where are you now?

1. What are 3 to 4 words or phrases that first come to mind when you see or hear the word leadership?

2. Read the following thoughts on leadership from various leaders:

The most dangerous leadership myth is that leaders are born-that there is a genetic factor to leadership. That's nonsense; in fact, the opposite is true. Leaders are made rather than born.

—Warren Bennis, American scholar and
pioneer in the field of Leadership Studies

I grew up in war and saw the United Nations help my country to recover and rebuild. That experience was a big part of what led me to pursue a career in public service. You have to work and think about how we can make this world a better place for all. This is what I'd really like to ask our young leaders. We will try as leaders of today to minimize the problems which we will hand over to you. But it is up to you. You have to take ownership and leadership of tomorrow. For that to be possible, you have to strengthen your capacity and widen your vision as a global citizen.

—Ban Ki-Moon, Secretary-General of the United Nations

Leadership is not defined by the exercise of power but by the capacity to increase the power among those who are led.

—Mary Parker Follett, The Creative Experience

Leadership is all about people. It is not about organizations. It is not about plans. It is not about strategies. It is all about people—motivating people to get the job done. You have to be people-centered.

—Colin Powell, Former U.S. Secretary of State

We hold ourselves back in ways both big and small, by lacking self-confidence, by not raising our hands, and by pulling back when we should be leaning in. Be ambitious not just in pursuing your dreams but in aspiring to become leaders in your fields.

—Sheryl Sandberg, COO Facebook

Leadership is the art of mobilizing others to want to struggle for shared aspirations.

—Jim Kouzes and Barry Posner,
authors of *The Leadership Challenge*

Use the space below to identify/explain which quotes are most impactful to you and why. Are there any you agree or disagree with?

3. How did the article "What Makes a Leader" by Daniel Goleman change or enhance your definition of leadership?

4. What were your main takeaways from the Emotional Intelligence assessment (EQ-i) you took? You can list both strengths and areas for development. (Graduate Students: you will not fill this part out until you have had a debrief meeting.)

5. What surprised you about these results? Feel free to include both what you liked and didn't like.

6. Ask **two** other people who know you well (e.g., mentor, supervisor, peer, co-worker, team member, friend) to each identify your top 2 interpersonal strengths and 1 opportunity for development.

   a. Source 1:
   b. Source 2:

Part 2

Envisioning Your Leadership Best Self: Where do you want to be?

(Note: Parts 2 and 3 are to be completed during the first meeting with your coach.)

1. Will you be involved in any organizations, clubs, or teams this semester, and what are your roles in each? How do you see yourself stepping up to lead/influence others in this context? Is there a new leadership opportunity that you are considering pursuing?

2. What is your vision of the kind of leader you want to be? What words or phrases would you want to have your peers use to describe you as a leader? In other words, describe your *leadership best self*.

3. What are the benefits to you and others if you reach these goals?

Part 3

Creating Your Action Plan: How will you get there?

1. State your specific leader development goal:

2. How would achieving this goal support your vision of your leadership best self?

3. What new behaviors will you demonstrate during this semester? What will people observe you doing differently?

4. What's it going to take for you to achieve this goal? What resources are available to you? What challenges might you face in pursuing this goal?

5. How committed are you to this goal? What is likely to happen if you don't achieve it?

"People who succeed at long-term goals never succeed alone. They build and nurture relationships around them that provide support, advice, and accountability. Without that supportive network, they'd never be able to regroup during difficult times and find the will to keep going. In a technologically driven society, when it's easier to text someone than look them in the eyes, some people have let important relationships lapse or haven't ever confessed their fears or goals to anyone who might be able to help them."

—Caroline Adams Miller, author of *Getting Grit*

Appendix 2: The Doerr Institute Core Leadership Competencies

The 21 Doerr Institute Core Leader Competencies are derived from contemporary research on leaders[143] and are organized into five broad, rationally derived themes. This list of competencies does not capture every skill that a leader might need to be successful. Rather, this list encapsulates a wide range of fundamental characteristics related to leader effectiveness that are especially appropriate for development within a college-aged population.

Themes:

Knowing Yourself

Leaders are aware of themselves and their values and purpose. They have the confidence to stand up for themselves and what they believe in.

Controlling Yourself

Leaders manage their emotions, behaviors, and time effectively. They work and make decisions well under pressure. Leaders maintain hope and focus, even in the face of setbacks.

Growing and Flourishing

Leaders desire to continue to learn and to develop new ideas. They cultivate a vision of what is possible and take the initiative to pursue new opportunities.

Being Aware of Others

Leaders listen to the perspectives of others, including people who are not like themselves. They seek to understand others and pursue the greater good.

Working with Others

Leaders work well with others. When conflict arises, they deal with it effectively. Leaders delegate when in groups and pursue the success of the team as a whole. They can influence others and can build successful cultures within their teams and groups.

Knowing Yourself

Purposefulness: Leaders show an awareness of their beliefs and adhere to a situationally appropriate and effective set of core values. They act in alignment with their values, which they tie to an articulated sense of purpose.

Self-Confidence: Leaders can maintain their position in the face of conflict with peers. They display self-assuredness without being aggressive when they assert their own perspective, position, beliefs, attitudes, and intentions. Leaders have the moral courage to speak up when they witness something wrong and the self-confidence to publicly praise others.

Self-Awareness: Leaders have a clear sense of their own needs, motives, strengths, and weaknesses while simultaneously being aware that they also have blind spots in their self-knowledge. This dual understanding promotes humility and strength and allows them to influence others but remain open to criticism and be non-defensive when receiving constructive feedback.

Controlling Yourself

Self-Regulation: Leaders interpret and manage their own moods, emotions, and behaviors. They are a stabilizing influence on peers in a crisis, respond to failure with renewed energy, and do not become emotionally overwhelmed when facing a challenge.

Balance: Leaders prioritize their goals, value time and use it effectively, and display physically and emotionally healthy work habits. They maintain a deliberate, complementary relationship between work and what they view as broadening experiences, social interactions, and play. Leaders are not one-dimensional, and they find purpose and meaning across multiple facets of life.

Decision-Making: Leaders make decisions in a timely manner, sometimes with incomplete information and under tight deadlines and pressure. Their decisions are grounded in reality and enhanced by relevant information sought from others. Leaders are able to make quick decisions when necessary based on both the information available and the likely consequences of decision outcomes.

Perseverance: Leaders drive toward task completion and, in most instances, do not quit before finishing, particularly when faced with setbacks, failure, or resistance. They express, through their behavior, a commitment to long-term goals, coupled with a sustained energy to achieve their objectives.

Growing and Flourishing

Innovative Thinking: Leaders think creatively, and they add value by creating original ideas and novel solutions by making connections among previously unrelated ideas.

Enterprising Initiative: Leaders exhibit the capacity and willingness to develop new ventures to respond to new opportunities and identified needs. They balance risks with potential rewards and are able to identify and manage the resources needed to develop new ventures and position them for success.

Love of Learning: Leaders hold internal motivations that drive the need for personal growth and the capacity to lead. They find meaning in their work and pursue excellence in the absence of external incentives. Leaders demonstrate intellectual curiosity and pursue learning for its own sake.

Vision Casting: Leaders maintain hope in the face of uncertainty and describe possibilities in ways that can inspire and motivate others. They use symbolism to articulate a vision and to rally support behind it. Leaders inspire themselves and others to make progress when the situation is complex and ambiguous by keeping their eyes fixed on their objectives.

Being Aware of Others

Cross-Cultural Resourcefulness: Leaders think globally when framing projects and problems, and they actively seek greater understanding of the perspectives of those whose cultures diverge from their own. Leaders participate with others across the social spectrum in order to be more creative, effective, and inclusive.

Ethical Responsibility: Leaders demonstrate an awareness of the needs of others, and they exhibit selflessness in pursuit of the greater good, according to the normative ethical standards of their culture. They consider and are influenced by the second- and third-order consequences of their decisions.

Empathic Engagement: Leaders show that they pay attention to others, that they listen patiently to what others have to say, and that they can accurately articulate the arguments or opinions of others, even when disagreeing with them. Leaders demonstrate empathy with the experiences and feelings of others, work actively to take the perspective of others, and extend their own influence by understanding others' perspectives. Leaders demonstrate the patience to hear people out without interrupting or talking over them.

Working with Others

Conflict Management: Leaders demonstrate a willingness to enter into conflict, seek to understand the nature of the conflict, and guide themselves and others to a common, accepted solution. Leaders do not run away from conflicts but approach them as opportunities. They demonstrate focused listening, can size up situations quickly, and drive for resolution and agreement.

Team-Building: Leaders create strong morale and a sense of belonging in a group of peers with a common goal. They share credit for successes, and they define success in terms of the whole team. Leaders respect the autonomy of peers and allow them to be responsible for their portion of a project.

Collaboration: Leaders demonstrate the ability to create partnerships to accomplish work, display candor and fairness in groups, and create conditions in which others want to work together. Leaders develop trust with others and resolve interpersonal problems with minimal disruption or conflict. They are skilled at finding common ground and representing their own interests while also being fair to others.

Delegation: Leaders delegate responsibilities to others in group work, allow others to finish their portion of the work without micromanaging, and trust others to perform.

Negotiation: Leaders gain the trust of others, understand the best alternatives to a negotiated agreement, accept necessary concessions, and lead others to arrangements that are mutually satisfying. They build rapport in ways that help their ideas gain traction and their goals to be achieved. Leaders influence others' perceptions so that they and others are satisfied with negotiated outcomes.

Development: Leaders actively assist others in the pursuit of their own growth. They know when to give advice, when to ask questions, and when to defer coaching and mentoring to others with greater skill or experience. Leaders are able to focus on the trajectory of others and not impose their own values on them.

Effective Communication: Leaders communicate clearly and powerfully in written, visual, and oral forms, whether with respect to technical data or abstract, socially sensitive issues. They can command attention and manage audiences with agility and flexibility. They are able to sense when communication is breaking down, engage in alternative communication strategies, and receive questions and criticisms without losing their composure.

Appendix 3: A Brief Primer on Using the Scientific Method to Evaluate Leader Development Programs

The Doerr Institute believes that for leader development in higher education (or anywhere else, for that matter) to move beyond "smiley sheets" and vague claims of efficacy into the 21st century, it must be evidence based and scientifically evaluated. Testing a program's objectives empirically is the only reliable way to know whether those objectives are being achieved. Because most social interventions fail to produce any significant changes in the human experience, and some actually produce the *opposite* of what they were designed to produce, it is critical that we carefully and rigorously evaluate the fruits of our labors when it comes to developing leaders. Doing so will allow us to course correct in a timely fashion, and it will save time and money in the long-term as we identify initiatives that are failing to produce results.

For those who wish to scientifically evaluate the efficacy of their leader development initiatives, we have written this research design and measurement primer to aid them in their efforts. Although some readers of this book will have all the training they need to evaluate a leader development program (in addition to understanding and critiquing the studies and data-based arguments that we make in this book), others might not. It is for the latter group that we have written this primer, which summarizes some basic issues in research methods and analysis that we think are fundamental to building an effective measurement system within a leader development program and to evaluating some of the claims that people make about their own leader development approach—including claims that we make in this book about ours.

We want to emphasize that the skills and training needed to create an effective measurement system like the one we discuss at length in this book can be found on virtually every major college and university campus in the United States. There is nothing unique or new about the measurement and research design concepts that we discuss in this appendix or elsewhere in this book. What *is* unique is the consistent application of these measurement and design concepts to a leader development program. Thus, we encourage readers coming from higher education to seek the expertise of social scientists on their campuses for assistance in designing a measurement system for their own leader development programs. That such programs should be rigorously measured and evaluated is one of the most important arguments we make in this book.

Research Design Fundamentals

When social scientists design studies to test hypotheses—such as the hypothesis that a particular intervention will help people become better leaders—they must answer a variety of questions before they begin in earnest. For instance, can they experimentally *manipulate* (through random assignment) the variables of interest, or can they only *measure* these variables (because it is not possible or practical or financially viable to manipulate them)? If they can manipulate the variables of interest, what is the best way to do that? If not, what sort of non-experimental design will result in the most useful information and get them as close as possible to the answers they most want? Those answers most often tend to involve cause and effect relationships, or what causes what in the universe of human experiences, but that isn't always the case. The best research design will always be preceded by the clear articulation of a researcher's objectives. So, be clear about what it is that you really need to know before you start designing studies to find out.

When what you most need to know is whether an intervention causes specific changes in people, the best research design to answer that question will be an experiment. However, there are a variety of experimental designs that you might use, and there are also some near-equivalent designs that can take you a long way toward your goal of knowing about cause and effect when a true experimental design is not feasible.

For example, if you were to design a program or intervention that people voluntarily participate in, you must be aware of the influence of *selection bias*, which results in people with certain characteristics engaging in your program or intervention. For example, if you were to design a smoking cessation program, you know immediately that the kind of person who will volunteer to participate is going to be someone who smokes. Indeed, if that weren't the case, you probably wouldn't allow them to participate! But "someone who smokes" isn't going to be the only special characteristic of the people who participate. Smokers, for instance, tend to be poorer and less educated than non-smokers, at least in the United States. They also tend to be less likely to exercise than the average non-smoker and less likely to eat healthy foods. Perhaps more important than all such characteristics, though, is that people who volunteer to participate in your smoking cessation program are likely to be people who want to stop smoking but have struggled to stop on their own. That means they are different not just from non-smokers but also from smokers who decide *not* to participate in your program.

These kinds of differences, all due to selection bias, make it important to design the right kind of study that is capable of telling you what you really need to know about the effectiveness of your program. If you know the percentage of smokers who succeed in quitting on their own, you might think that all you have to do is beat this number in order to determine that your program is effective in helping people quit smoking. But that isn't really true. What you would need to do is to document that people who participate in your program successfully quit smoking at higher rates than the same type of person who doesn't participate in your program. In other words, you need the right kind of comparison group.

What if the kind of people who volunteer to participate in your smoking cessation program are different in another way? What if they are the kind of people who are so strongly motivated to quit smoking that they will go to the trouble to sign up for a formal program like yours? That could mean that you wouldn't have to do anything special to them at all, and they would still be likely to quit. You could just feed them raw broccoli every time they show up to your office, and they would end up quitting smoking at higher rates than non-smokers. That doesn't mean that giving people broccoli helps them quit smoking. It just means that you've "discovered" that motivation matters when it comes to quitting a bad habit, and you've managed to attract highly motivated people. Congratulations.

This example makes a good parallel to what we typically see with voluntary leader development programs on college campuses. What kind of person is most likely to participate in such programs? The answer might differ from one campus to another, and it might differ within the same campus from one time point to the next. If you want to know whether your program is helping people to become better leaders, you would do well to design an experiment (or at least a quasi-experiment) to find out. When you do, selection bias will be a major challenge to contend with.

Waitlist Control Design

Perhaps the very best experimental design you could use to test the effectiveness of your leader development program involves what researchers call a "waitlist control group design." This type of design deals with the pesky problem of selection bias in a simple but powerful way. In this design, you take a group of people that volunteers for a leader development experience, and you randomly assign those people to either go through the developmental experience immediately or to wait for a specified period of time to do so. The latter group is your waitlisted control group. Importantly, all participants, no matter what group they are assigned to, must complete your outcome measures at the same point in time. In a "pre-post waitlist-controlled experiment," everyone in the study will complete the outcome measures twice—once before and once after the experimental period. This is the most powerful type of experimental design to determine the effectiveness of a training program or intervention, as it deals most effectively with the problems of selection bias that we have been discussing and works well even with relatively modest sample sizes (because of the pre-post element of the design).

Using a pre-post waitlist-controlled experiment like this, researchers could definitively determine whether an intervention caused changes in people's ability to lead (assuming they had measured the right outcomes; we will have more to say on that matter shortly). This design allows researchers to know whether any changes in the outcomes that they observe in the group that received the intervention would have happened anyway, even without the intervention, simply because of the kind of people who volunteered to participate in the program in question.

We should also note that in the very best waitlist-controlled experimental design, the waitlisted group gets to experience something that sounds, feels, and smells something like the real intervention (you might think of this as a sort of "placebo experience") but that lacks the essence of what makes the intervention "real." However, this kind of design element often requires a degree of deception that will be problematic in many contexts, both for ethical reasons and because lying to people who showed up at your door to be developed has a tendency to breed resentment when people eventually find out they have been deceived. That's not something most leader development programs can afford, if they want to remain in business for a long time. Thus, having the waitlisted group simply wait is often the only viable option in most contexts.

If giving people the same outcome measures both before and after an intervention is not feasible, the next best design would be a waitlist-controlled experiment in which everyone only completes the outcome measures once, at the end of the intervention period. Such a design necessitates having a large group to begin with. (By large, we mean something on the order of 100 to 200 people in total, although the "right" number depends on a host of factors, including the magnitude of the effects of the intervention itself and the precision of the outcome measures used to assess the intervention's effects).

Quasi-Experimental Designs

Often, researchers won't have the luxury of conducting a waitlist-controlled experiment. In such cases, other designs might still be feasible and can offer a reasonable alternative to such an experiment. Perhaps the best such alternative design involves finding or creating an appropriately matched comparison group against which the outcomes assessed in the intervention group can be contrasted. In such "quasi-experimental" designs, it is ideal to measure the outcomes twice—both before and after the intervention time period. This pre-post measurement approach reveals whether the intervention group and the comparison group were different from the outset of the study or if they were reasonably equivalent at the start (but, ideally, not equivalent at the end).

Internal Reference Group Design

What do you do when you can't find or create a reasonably equivalent comparison group? In many applied contexts involving training-type interventions, well-matched comparison groups can be difficult to come by, and in such situations, there is a good option that can be used to evaluate the effectiveness of an intervention. This alternative to using a comparison group, known as an internal reference group design, involves creating an outcome or set of outcomes that should not be responsive to the intervention (so, you would not expect to see any changes on these measures) and using these outcome measures essentially as a measurement-level comparison group. In this design, you only have one group of people in your study, and this group all participates in the training or intervention experience. What are compared in this design are changes (from pre to post) in the intervention-relevant outcomes as well as changes in the intervention-irrelevant outcomes. If larger changes occur in the former group than in the latter, you can be reasonably confident that the training or intervention caused those changes. A waitlist-controlled experiment would, of course, be a better design, but an internal reference group design is far superior to nothing at all when a waitlist-controlled experiment isn't an option.

Measuring Outcomes

Even if you are able to design the ideal study for assessing the effectiveness of a leader development initiative, that study will be useless without the right outcome measures. This element of the evaluation process is absolutely critical, and it is an element on which we tend to spend a great deal of time and effort at the Doerr Institute, especially when we design studies to evaluate new programs.

In the process of creating or finding appropriate outcome measures to evaluate a leader development initiative, or any other type of training program, there are three broad principles that we would urge you to consider. These are principles that we bear in mind every time we evaluate a leader development initiative.

First, there is not one "right" way to measure outcomes in this space. The best outcome measures will always be tailored to the specific goals of each initiative. Form must always follow function when it comes to measurement. Furthermore, it is important that we not rely 100% on any single measure or method. Thus, for example, asking trainees to report their attitudes or beliefs on a survey before and after training is a perfectly valid way to capture attitudes and beliefs. In fact, asking people what they think and feel is the BEST way to find out what they think and feel. It's not necessarily the best way to capture their behaviors, however, which might be better evaluated using methods such as expert observations, peers ratings, or even objective behavioral indices. If a training initiative is designed to change behaviors first and foremost, then behavioral measures are a necessity for the effective measurement of that initiative. If a training initiative is designed to change attitudes, beliefs, or personal identity, in contrast, then behavioral measures might be almost irrelevant to a proper measurement system.

Second, although specific measures used to evaluate a leader development initiative ought to fit the specific objectives of each program, in general we should be sure to include measures of *affect* (emotions), *cognitions* (thoughts—about the self, others, and concepts like leadership), and *behaviors* in our measurement repertoire, as these three domains arguably comprise the whole of the human experience from a social-scientific perspective. Thus, whereas measures of affect are not intrinsically better or worse than measures of behavior and one type of measure might be more appropriate for a particular training initiative, both types of measures should be used across the span of a comprehensive measurement system. Otherwise, an important dimension of the human experience will be missed.

Third and finally, it is important to measure changes in affect, cognition, and behavior in both *proximal* and *distal* ways. At the Doerr Institute, we typically measure changes pre and post training, with the post measures usually occurring within two weeks of the completion of an intervention. Such measures are proximal measures that are designed to maximize the opportunity to capture any changes that might have occurred in trainees. But our ultimate goal is not to produce fleeting, short-term changes in emerging leaders. What we want to see are changes that "stick" and produce a trajectory shift for students who work with us to develop their capacity to lead. Consequently, we measure changes in the short term when evaluating a particular program, and we might subsequently use the same measures at a later date to evaluate whether proximal changes remain significant over time. But we might also use completely different measures to evaluate the long-term, distal impact of our leader development initiatives. What is important is that we know whether changes occur soon after a developmental experience, and whether we can see lasting changes in the long term as well.

For instance, throughout this book we have described our use of a simple measure of leader identity, and we have discussed ways in which we can see that leader identity scores on this measure change following such interventions as professional leadership coaching. But we have also created a more distal measure of the impact of our work with students—what we call the "emergent leadership experience" (or ELE) score. An ELE score captures all of the formal leadership roles that students can take on campus, which we have coded for the levels of leadership responsibility that each role entails. Although no particular program at the Doerr Institute is designed to encourage students to take on formal leadership roles while at Rice University, we would hope that students who feel more capable of leading well (as their elevated scores on our leader identity measure typically indicate) would translate their confidence into action and that other students would perceive their capabilities and support them as leaders.

Our evidence to date suggests that this is, in fact, what happens. Specifically, students who work with the Doerr Institute enhance their leader identities (their sense that they are leaders, their confidence that they can lead effectively, and their desire to take on leadership roles), and we have found that leader identity is positively associated with higher ELE scores over time. We have also found that short-term, proximal changes in leader identity remain significantly changed one to three years after students graduate from Rice. Thus, we have evidence of short-term (proximal) changes in leader identity following our work with students, as well as more distal evidence that these short-term changes "stick" for several years. We also have evidence for additional but related distal outcomes (ELE scores) that complement the short-term evidence and give us greater confidence that our interventions are producing the kinds of meaningful, long-term effects that they are designed to produce.

The measurement process at the Doerr Institute always begins with the articulation of the precise objectives of a training or development program. "What are you hoping will change?" is the fundamental question the measurement team asks the leader development team when it designs a new program. Often, the replies to this question start off somewhat broad and perhaps even a little vague, but with repeated questioning and clarifying (e.g., "Yes, but what do you really mean by that?"), the measurement team is able to zero-in on the right objectives and begin to search for, or create, measures that fit these objectives.

When researchers create a new measure, or when they evaluate an existing measure for its potential to assess a new program, there are several fundamental issues that they will tend to consider, including the following:

1. Is the measure reliable? Reliability concerns the extent to which a measure is consistent, which can be evaluated, typically, in three distinct ways. The first way is its consistency over time, sometimes called "test-retest" reliability, which indicates the degree to which scores on a measure taken at one point in time are correlated with scores from the same people on the same measure at a later point in time. The second way to evaluate reliability is through its internal consistency, which concerns the extent to which the multiple items on a scale are correlated with one another. A third way to evaluate reliability that is specific to measures that depend on multiple observers to rate the same behavior, skill, or target outcome, concerns the extent to which the measure exhibits "inter-rater reliability." Test-retest reliability and inter-rater reliability (when there are only two raters involved) can be measured with a simple correlation coefficient (r) from time 1 to time 2, whereas internal consistency is typically measured with Cronbach's alpha (a) or a similar statistical test.

2. Is the measure valid? Validity is, arguably, the most important aspect of a measure, and in this context, it concerns the extent to which scores on a measure truly reflect the variable, or idea, that the measure is meant to capture. Like reliability, validity can be subdivided into several different types. For example, face validity reflects the extent to which the measure appears to capture the construct it is supposed to capture "on its face." Criterion validity reflects the extent to which a measure is correlated with other variables that are conceptually related, including measures of the same construct but also extending to measures of other, related constructs. Criterion validity can be assessed concurrently (all measures are evaluated at the same point in time) or predictively (measures are evaluated at different points in time). Finally, a valid measure will also exhibit discriminant validity, which refers to the extent to which a measure is not associated with measures of constructs that are conceptually unrelated to the construct the focal measure is supposed to capture.

These criteria of reliability and validity are important dimensions on which to evaluate the quality of a measure, whether it is one that we find in the research literature or one that we create ourselves. But equally important is what we mentioned earlier—the fit between the objectives of a particular program whose impact we wish to measure and the content, type, and method of measurement. It is worth repeating that if the measure we choose does not really fit the objectives of the intervention in question, then none of the data we will gather will amount to anything. No fancy, complex statistical machinations can make up for a failure to gather the right data in the first place. For a great example of the use of these concepts to evaluate a set of measures in the specific realm of "cross-cultural competence," see the 2013 paper by Matsumoto and Hwang referenced at the end of this appendix.

Statistical Analysis of Data

So, you've decided to measure the impact of your leader development program. Well done. After making that important decision, you designed a study appropriate to your context and resources, determined what your program objectives are, found (or created) a measure that fit those objectives, and gathered your data. What now?

Now you analyze the data to find out if your objectives were achieved. For data nerds, this is the really fun part, like the part of the adventure story where the hero has followed the map that leads to the buried treasure and begins to dig, hoping for riches.

This primer is not designed to turn lay people into statisticians. It's here to assist knowledgeable readers in their thinking about what it takes to implement an effective measurement system that is capable of telling them what they need to know about whether or not a leader development initiative is working. With this broad goal in view, we will not go into a great deal of detail about the mechanics of statistical analysis, but we do want to mention a few important principles that even non-statisticians will find valuable, whether they are thinking about their own data or other people's data.

Perhaps the most important thing to keep in mind is the statistical meaning of the word, "significance." This word, which we use throughout this book, indicates that a finding (such as the difference between a trained group and a non-trained group or the association between two variables) is unlikely to be a chance occurrence or random fluke. As such, labeling a result as statistically significant is extremely important. After all, only results that are statistically significant can be heralded as scientific evidence in support of a claim that a program works.

Without delving into a great deal of math or discussing the essence of probability theory, it is worth taking a moment to understand what statistical significance depends upon. Consider the following conceptual formula:

$$\text{Significance} = \text{effect size } ' \text{ sample size}$$

What this equation indicates is that a result will be statistically significant when it is based on an effect that is large, even if the sample size used to evaluate the effect is small, or when the effect is actually somewhat small but the sample size is large. A tiny effect, in other words, might still be labeled as statistically significant if it comes from a huge sample (e.g., 1,000 respondents to a survey or 10,000 test scores). When you design a program to help people become better leaders, you should make sure that your claims of efficacy depend on statistically significant results of carefully designed studies by following the kinds of principles that we have described in this appendix.

However, two caveats are important to keep in mind. First, a result can be statistically significant without being practically significant. What this means is that a program might produce real (i.e., non-chance) effects on people's ability to lead, but if the size of that effect is pretty small, you have to ask whether it is worth the effort that it takes to create it. Second, a large effect that comes from a small sample might be statistically significant, but the small sample size from which it derives should still be a cause for concern. Large effects that come from small samples are often unreliable, meaning that if we attempted to replicate them, we might not find the same results a second time.

What does all of this mean in a practical sense? It means that when we evaluate the effects of an intervention, we need to keep all three of these dimensions in mind: statistical significance (is the effect real?), effect size (is the effect big enough to care about?), and sample size (is the sample big enough that it is not likely to be unusual in some important way but is instead likely to be fairly representative of the population from which it was taken?). At the Doerr Institute, when we gather pre and post data on the same people (before and after training), we do not typically draw conclusions about the effectiveness of an intervention without having data from at least 20, and preferably 30, individuals. If we are comparing groups of people and only have data after training has occurred (so, only post data with no pre data), then we do not typically draw any firm conclusions about the effectiveness of an intervention without at least 50 people (in each group that we are comparing). At sample sizes as small as 20–50 people, statistically significant results aren't going to occur unless effect sizes are medium to large (indicating a fair degree of practical significance), but we can still be reasonably confident that a significant result can be replicated.

As an additional safeguard against drawing false conclusions about the benefits of a developmental intervention (what statisticians often refer to as a "type I error"), we almost always include multiple outcome measures when we evaluate a program. A result that is significant but comes from a small, unusual sample is less likely to be accompanied by *another* significant result on an independent outcome, as a general rule. Of course, the best way to make sure that a result is reliable is to replicate it, which is also something that we like to do as often as possible, especially with outcome measures that do not demand a great deal of resources (such as self-report measures, including measures of leader identity, self-concept clarity, humility, and sense of purpose, among others described in this book) and findings that are especially remarkable or important.

For Further Reading

Readers interested in learning more about the concepts that we have discussed in this appendix are encouraged to explore the following works, which are rich and readable sources of information about research design principles and statistical reasoning:

Lawson, T. J. *Everyday Statistical Reasoning*. Pacific Grove, CA: Wadsworth, 2002.

Matsumoto, D., and H.C. Hwang. "Assessing Cross-Cultural Competence: A Review of Available Tests. *Journal of Cross-Cultural Psychology* 44 (2002): 849–73.

Shadish, W., T Cook, and D. Campbell. *Experimental and Quasi-Experimental Designs for Generalized Causal Inference*. Boston, MA: Houghton Mifflin, 2002.

Appendix 4: Framework for the Classification on Leadership for a Public Purpose

The framework for the Leadership for Public Purpose classification makes this goal a desired institutional outcome of colleges and universities. It reflects institutional missions that claim to positively impact society. Effective leadership for public purpose transcends functional or instrumental leadership (i.e., personal career or political gain or narrow business or organization outcomes) in pursuit of collective public goods like justice, equity, diversity, and liberty. Leadership for public purpose can be manifest in all realms of social life—private business, public and nonprofit institutions, neighborhood and community life, professional associations, civil and government institutions, religious institutions, and more. Institutions earning the Carnegie classification will demonstrate a commitment to leadership for a public purpose through their investments in leader development; development of ethical and moral judgement; and development of the critical thinking necessary to understand systemic and cultural aspects of power and privilege within which all leadership resides.

Campuses that are committed to leadership for public purpose enhance the learning, teaching, and research mission of their institution by: developing leadership abilities in all institutional stakeholders; contributing to the public scholarly understanding of leadership as a public good and the sociopolitical contexts, systems, and practices within which all leadership resides; and preparing students for lives of leadership for public purpose in their careers, communities, and the broader society.

Throughout the application, schools will have the opportunity to answer all the sections that are applicable to their campus and context in order to provide evidence of their commitment to leadership for a public purpose. No single question will be used as a litmus test to achieve the designation, but campuses will be encouraged to undergo a process of self-evaluation by whichever process they find more effective. The sections found throughout the application are:

I.   **Foundational Indicators**
Foundational indicators are those that best illustrate a broad and deep commitment to leadership for public purpose in the institution's policies, operating norms, and routines, as well as organizational activities and practices. Subsections include:

a. **Institutional Identity and Culture**
Sample question: Describe how leadership is explicitly a part of your institutional mission or vision. Use direct quotes from the mission and vision as evidence.

b. **Institutional Communication**
Sample question: Describe how the institution emphasizes leadership for a public purpose as part of its brand message. For example, in public marketing materials, websites, or admissions packets.

c. **Institutional Infrastructure and Resource Allocations**
Sample question: Describe the structure, staffing, and purpose of the coordinating infrastructure (e.g., center, office, network or coalition of centers) for leadership on your campus. If the campus has more than one center coordinating leadership, describe each center, staffing, and purpose and indicate how the multiple centers interact with one another to advance institutional commitment to leadership.

d. **Human Resources**
Sample question: Describe the professional development for employees related to leadership that is provided or supported by the institution. Provide examples (e.g., workshops, mentoring, self-directed learning resources, courses).

e. **Institutional Assessment**
Sample question: Describe systematic campus-wide assessment mechanisms to measure the outcomes and impact of the institutional commitment to leadership.

f. **Institutional Alignment**
Sample question: Describe how the institution's commitment to leadership for a public purpose directly contributes to student recruitment.

II. **Leadership Curriculum**
Curricular leadership is integrated into credit-bearing coursework. Curricular leadership may approach leadership from a wide variety of theoretical and educational perspectives (e.g., leader develop-

ment, study of leaders, systems of leadership, leadership in cultural context).

Sample Question: Describe the availability of leadership courses to students.

III. **Leadership Co-Curriculum**

Co-curricular leadership is integrated into the non-credit-bearing educational activities of the institution. In order for an educational activity to be considered co-curricular it must have well-articulated learning outcomes, clearly structured and developmental approach to learning, and assessment of student learning. Social or extracurricular activities that do not have these essential elements are not co-curricular.

Sample question: Describe the availability of co-curricular leadership offerings to students.

IV. **Leadership Pedagogy**

Leadership pedagogy is educational methodology in curricular and co-curricular leadership offerings.

Sample question: Describe the training and professional development required of any faculty member offering leadership courses and/or co-curricular leadership offerings.

V. **Leadership Scholarship**

Leadership scholarship and professional activity reflects the creation of new knowledge about leadership in post-secondary institutions.

Sample question: Describe how the knowledge produced through scholarship and professional activities focused on leadership is used in the institution.

Campuses that complete the application will undergo a transformative self-examination of their current practices, policies, and institutional approach to leadership education and development. Once campuses submit their applications, a panel of expert reviewers will evaluate each one by considering their answers in alignment with their context and subsequently offer their recommendation on awarding the designation of Leadership for Public Purpose.

To access the full application and join the Leadership Reckoning, go to www.doerr.rice.edu.

Acknowledgments

For their generosity to Rice University and their vision in creating the Doerr Institute for New Leaders, we are immensely appreciative to Ann and John Doerr. The Doerr Insitute itself would probably never have gotten out of the "good idea" stage if it were not for the administrative genius of Lillie Besozzi, who started the Institute with Tom Kolditz in the summer of 2015, as well as John Strackhouse of Caldwell Partners, who recruited Tom and provided pro bono recruitment of our incredible External Advisory Board that includes Vice President Al Gore, Secretary Colin Powell, Professor Klaus Schwab, Jim Collins, Carolyn Miles, Wendy Kopp, and David Rhodes. We are indebted to our current and former Fellows, Annise Parker, Ed Emmett, Bruce Avolio, David Day, Jim Kouzes, Tae Kouzes, Dr. Mathew Johnson, and Dr. Vida Yao, all of whom have brought a wealth of experience and knowledge to bear on our behalf, much of it showing up in the pages of this book. And we are especially grateful to colleagues at the Carnegie Foundation for the Advancement of Teaching—Mathew Johnson, Paul LeMahieu, and Gene Corbin—for helping us to formulate a workable improvement strategy for leadership development and education in higher education, and for public purpose. The Rice University staff and faculty deserve special mention, as they took in stride the disruption that IS the Doerr Institute, always helping and encouraging us as a start-up, never engaging in the insecure pettiness that often emerges in institutions that undergo substantial change. Current and former members of our Faculty Advisory Board are too numerous to list individually, but they represent the finest supporters among our faculty.

None of the work that we discuss in this book would be worth talking about were it not for the tireless efforts and immense professionalism of our friends and colleagues at the Doerr Institute, including Stephanie Taylor, Sarah Sullivan, Chase Crook, Brooklyn Holt, and Marcel Fingers, in addition to the current and past postdoctoral research fellows who have added their creativity and brilliance to the Institute over the years (Dr. Lebena Varghese, Dr. Carla Ortega-Santori, and Dr. Cody Bok). A host of graduate students and faculty members at Rice University have also served the Institute beautifully from its founding to the present, and we remain in their debt.

A special thanks is owed to Ruth Reitmeier, assistant director of coaching at the Doerr Institute, who read every word of the initial draft of this book and helped make our prose clearer and more effective. Likewise, Dr. Carla Ortega-Santori provided an excellent summary of the application process related to the Carnegie elective classification for Leadership for Public Purpose, which we included as Appendix 4 of this book.

Recognition is likewise due to Christina Hicks and her team at Monocle Press and to Kristen Foht, editor extraordinaire, whose patience and precision made this book actually readable for humans.

Finally, we gratefully acknowledge the support of our families, especially Kay, David, and Catherine, without whose love and support a book like this would never come to be, for we would not be who we are without them.

Endnotes

1   Jim Collins, *Good to Great: Why Some Companies Make the Leap…
and Others Don't* (New York: HarperBusiness, 2001).

2   Jim Collins, *Good to Great and the Social Sectors: Why Business
Thinking Is Not the Answer* (New York: HarperCollins, 2005).

3   "2018 Edelman Trust Barometer," Edelman, January 21, 2018,
https://www.edelman.com/research/2018-edelman-trust-barometer.

4   Cary Funk, "Mixed Messages about Public Trust in Science,"
Pew Research Center Science & Society, Pew Research Center, August
27, 2020, https://www.pewresearch.org/science/2017/12/08/mixed-mes-
sages-about-public-trust-in-science.

5   Matthew Harrington, "For the First Time in 17 Years, People's
Trust Declined in Every Kind of Institution We Asked About," *Harvard
Business Review*, April 11, 2017, https://hbr.org/2017/01/survey-peo-
ples-trust-has-declined-in-business-media-government-and-ngos.

6   Edelman, "Trust Barometer."

7   Sophie Cousins, "Measles: A Global Resurgence," *The Lancet* 19,
no. 4 (2019): 362–3.

8   Lauran Neegaard and Hannah Fingerhut, "AP-NORC Poll:
Half of Americans Would Get a COVID-19 Vaccine," *Associated
Press*, May 27, 2020, https://apnews.com/dacdc8bc428dd4df6511b-
fa259cfec44.

9   Cary Funk, Meg Hefferon, Brian Kennedy, and Courtney
Johnson, "Americans Generally View Medical Professionals Favorably, but About Half Consider Misconduct a Big Problem," Pew
Research Center, August 2, 2019, https://www.pewresearch.org/sci-
ence/2019/08/02/americans-generally-view-medical-professionals-fa-
vorably-but-about-half-consider-misconduct-a-big-problem.

10   B. J. Almond, "Ann and John Doerr Donate $50M to Devel-
op New Leaders at Rice," Rice News, May 14, 2015, http://news.rice.
edu/2015/05/14/ann-and-john-doerr-donate-50m-to-develop-new-
leaders-at-rice-university/.

11   "Our Roaring 20s: 'The Defining Decade,'" *NPR*, April 22,
2012, https://www.npr.org/2012/04/22/150429128/our-roaring-20s-
the-defining-decade.

12   "What Yale Looks For," Yale College Undergraduate Admissions,
accessed January 9, 2019, https://admissions.yale.edu/what-yale-looks-for.

13   "Rice University," Rice University, Office of Proposal Development, accessed January 10, 2019, https://opd.rice.edu/boilerplate-mate-
rials/rice-university.

14   Celina Pelaez Arias, "World Domination: 10 Best Schools for
Student Leaders," *College Magazine*, August 18, 2015, https://www.
collegemagazine.com/world-domination-cms-top-10-schools-future-
leaders.

15   U.S. News Staff, "2019 Best Colleges Preview: Top 25 National
Universities," *U.S. News & World Report*, September 7, 2018, https://
www.usnews.com/education/best-colleges/articles/2018-09-07/2019-
best-colleges-preview-top-25-national-universities.

16   Tara Isabella Burton, "Why Are American Colleges Obsessed
With 'Leadership'?" *The Atlantic*, January 22, 2014, https://www.theat-
lantic.com/education/archive/2014/01/why-are-american-colleges-ob-
sessed-with-leadership/283253/.

17   U.S. News Staff, "2019 Best Colleges Preview."

18   Arias, "World Domination."

19   John Byrne, "How Much Attention Should You Pay to U.S.
News' College Rankings?" *Forbes*, September 10, 2018, https://www.
forbes.com/sites/poetsandquants/2018/09/10/how-much-attention-
should-you-pay-to-u-s-news-college-rankings/#1bb3f257daf7.

20   Scott Jaschik, "Oklahoma Gave False Data for Years to 'U.S.
News,' Loses Ranking," Inside Higher Ed, May 28, 2019, https://www.
insidehighered.com/admissions/article/2019/05/28/university-oklaho-
ma-stripped-us-news-ranking-supplying-false.

21   Jeffrey Jensen Arnett, "Emerging Adulthood: A Theory of Development from the Late Teens Through the Twenties," *American Psychologist* 55, no. 5 (2000): 469–80.

22   Arnett, "Emerging Adulthood."

23   Robert M. Saposky, *Behave: The Biology of Humans at Our Best
and Worst* (New York: Penguin Books, 2017).

24   Timothy A. Salthouse, "Mediation of Adult Age Differences in
Cognition by Reductions in Working Memory and Speed of Processing," *Psychological Science* 2, no. 3 (1991): 179–83.

25   Sanjay Srivastava et al., "Development of Personality in Early
and Middle Adulthood: Set Like Plaster or Persistent Change?" *Journal
of Personality and Social Psychology* 84, no. 5 (2003): 1041–53.

26   See, for instance, Joyce E. Bono and Timothy A. Judge, "Personality and Transformational and Transactional Leadership: A Meta-Analysis," *Journal of Applied Psychology* 89, no. 5 (2004): 901–10.

27   Srivastava et al., "Development."

28   Ferris Jabr, "The Neuroscience of 20-Somethings," *Scientific American*, August 29, 2012, https://blogs.scientificamerican.com/brainwaves/the-neuroscience-of-twenty-somethings.

29   Sara B. Johnson, Robert W. Blum, and Jay N. Giedd, "Adolescent Maturity and the Brain: The Promise and Pitfalls of Neuroscience Research in Adolescent Health Policy," *Journal of Adolescent Health* 45, no. 3 (September 2009): 216–21, https://www.ncbi.nlm.nih.gov/pmc/articles/PMC2892678.

30   Robert G. Lord et al., "Leadership in Applied Psychology: Three Waves of Theory and Research," *Journal of Applied Psychology* 102, no. 3 (2017): 434–51.

31   Robert B. Kaiser and Gordy Curphy, "Leadership Development: The Failure of an Industry and the Opportunity for Consulting Psychologists," *Consulting Psychology Journal: Practice and Research* 65, no. 4 (2013): 294–302.

32   Ryan P. Brown and Lebena Varghese, "Holding Higher Education to Account: Measuring What Matters in the Development of Students as Leaders," *Journal of Character and Leadership Development* 6, no. 2 (2019): 33–48.

33   Nathan J. Hiller, "An Examination of Leadership Beliefs and Leadership Self-Identity: Constructs, Correlates, and Outcomes" (PhD diss., The Pennsylvania State University, 2005).

34   Brown and Varghese, "Measuring What Matters."

35   Richard Arvey et al., "Developmental and Genetic Determinants of Leadership Role Occupancy in Women," *Journal of Applied Psychology* 92, no. 3 (2007): 693–706.

36   George C. Thornton and William Byham, *Assessment Centers and Managerial Performance* (New York: Academic Press, 1982).

37   GoodReads, "William Faulkner Quotes," accessed January 7, 2019, https://www.goodreads.com/quotes/79715-in-writing-you-must-kill-all-your-darlings.

38   Jonathan Wai and Heiner Rindermann, "What Goes Into High Educational and Occupational Achievement? Education, Brains, Hard Work, Networks, and Other Factors," *High Ability Studies* 28 (2017): 127–45.

39   John Doerr, *Measure What Matters: How Google, Bono, and the Gates Foundation Rock the World with OKRs* (New York: Portfolio/Penguin, 2018).

40   Doerr, *Measure What Matters*, 251.

41   Sarah Payne, "93% of Managers Need Training on Coaching Employees," Workhuman, March 21, 2017, https://www.workhuman.com/resources/globoforce-blog/survey-93-of-managers-need-training-on-coaching-employees.

42   Forbes Coaches Council, "15 Trends That Will Redefine Executive Coaching in the Next Decade," *Forbes*, April 9, 2018, https://www.forbes.com/sites/forbescoachescouncil/2018/04/09/15-trends-that-will-redefine-executive-coaching-in-the-next-decade/#76b5911d6fc9.

43   Connie Whittaker Dunlop and Forbes Coaches Council, "The Success and Failure of the Coaching Industry," *Forbes*, October 5, 2017, https://www.forbes.com/sites/forbescoachescouncil/2017/10/05/the-success-and-failure-of-the-coaching-industry/#3aa42c666765.

44   Dunlop and Forbes Coaches Council, "Success and Failure."

45   "Credential Updates," International Coach Federation, accessed August 21, 2020, https://coachfederation.org/credential-updates.

46   "Types of Coaching," ICF Houston Chapter, accessed August 21, 2020, https://icfhoustoncoaches.org/Types_of_Coaching.

47   Anthony M. Grant, Linley Curtayne, and Geraldine Burton, "Executive Coaching Enhances Goal Attainment, Resilience and Workplace Well-Being: A Randomised Controlled Study," *The Journal of Positive Psychology* 4, no. 5 (2009): 396–407.

48   "About ICF," International Coach Federation, accessed August 21, 2020, https://coachfederation.org/about.

49   See, for example, Katherine Ely et al., "Evaluating Leadership Coaching: A Review and Integrated Framework," *The Leadership Quarterly* 21 (2010): 585–99.

50   Edgar H. Schein, *Humble Inquiry: The Gentle Art of Asking Instead of Telling* (San Francisco: Berrett-Koehler Publishers, 2013).

51   For example, see the meta-analysis by Rebecca Jones, Steven A. Woods, and Yves R. Guillaume, "The Effectiveness of Workplace Coaching: A Meta-Analysis of Learning and Performance Outcomes from Coaching," *Journal of Occupational and Organizational Psychology* 89, no. 2 (2016): 249–77.

52   Daniel Burt and Zenobia Talati, "The Unsolved Value of Executive Coaching: A Meta-Analysis of Outcomes Using Randomized Control Trial Studies," *International Journal of Evidence Based Coaching and Mentoring* 15, no. 2 (2017): 17–24.

53   Christina N. Lacerenza et al., "Leadership Training Design, Delivery, and Implementation: A Meta-Analysis," *Journal of Applied Psychology* 102, no. 12 (2017): 1686–718.

54   Stratford Sherman and Alyssa Freas, "The Wild West of Executive Coaching," *Harvard Business Review*, November 2004, https://hbr.org/2004/11/the-wild-west-of-executive-coaching.

55   Sherman and Freas, "Wild West."

56   Forbes Coaches Council, "15 Trends."

57   Payne, "93% of Managers."

58   Eric Schmidt, Jonathan Rosenber, and Alan Eagle, *Trillion Dollar Coach: The Leadership Playbook of Silicon Valley's Bill Campbell* (New York: Harper Business, 2019), 188.

59   Melissa Harrell and Lauren Barbato, "Great Managers Still Matter: The Evolution of Google's Project Oxygen," February 27, 2018, https://rework.withgoogle.com/blog/the-evolution-of-project-oxygen.

60   Victoria Mattingly and Kurt Kraiger, "Can Emotional Intelligence Be Trained? A Meta-Analytical Investigation," *Human Resource Management Review* 29, no. 2 (2019): 140–55.

61   Ryan P. Brown and Lebena Varghese, "Holding Higher Education to Account: Measuring What Matters in the Development of Students as Leaders," *Journal of Character and Leadership Development* 6, no. 2 (2019): 33–48.

62   See David V. Day, Michelle M. Harrison, Stanley M. Halpin, *An Integrative Approach to Leader Development: Connecting Adult Development, Identity, and Expertise* (New York: Taylor & Francis, 2009).

63   Robert G. Lord and Rosalie J. Hall, "Identity, Deep Structure and the Development of Leadership Skill," *The Leadership Quarterly* 16, no. 4 (2005): 591–615.

64   Day, Harrison, and Halpin, *Integrative Approach.*

65   Darja Miscenko, Hannes Guenter, and David V. Day, "Am I a Leader? Examining Leader Development Over Time," *The Leadership Quarterly* 28, no. 5 (2017): 605–20.

66   Miscenko, Guenter, and Day, "Am I a Leader?" p. 605.

67   Herminia Ibarra, *Act Like a Leader, Think Like a Leader* (Boston: HBR Press, 2015), 4.

68   Ibarra, *Act Like a Leader,* 4.

69   Katherine L. Yeager and Jamie L. Callahan, "Learning to Lead: Foundations of Emerging Leader Identity Development," *Advances in Developing Human Resources* 18, no. 3 (2016): 286–300.

70   Bruce J. Avolio and Gretchen R. Vogelgesang, "Beginnings Matter in Genuine Leadership Development," in *Early Development and Leadership: Building the Next Generation of Leaders*, eds. Susan Elaine Murphy and Rebecca J. Reichard (New York: Taylor & Francis, 2011), 179.

71   Yeager and Callahan, "Learning to Lead," 297.

72   Peter Salovey and John Mayer, "Emotional Intelligence," *Imagination, Cognition, and Personality* 9, no. 3 (1990): 185–211.

73   Daniel Goleman, *Emotional Intelligence: Why It Can Matter More Than IQ* (New York: Bantam Books, 1995).

74   See, for instance, Ryan P. Brown and Eric Anthony Day, "The Difference Isn't Black and White: Stereotype Threat and the Race Gap on Raven's Advanced Progressive Matrices," *Journal of Applied Psychology* 91, no. 4 (2006): 979–85.

75   For examples, see Loise Erlenmeyer-Kimling and Lissy F. Jarvik, "Genetics and Intelligence: A Review," *Science* 142, no. 3598 (1963): 1477–79; Cyril Burt, "The Genetic Determination of Differences in Intelligence: A Study of Monozygotic Twins Reared Together and Apart," *British Journal of Psychology* 57, no. 1-2 (1966): 137–53; Robert J. Sternberg, "Intelligence," in *Handbook of Psychology: History of Psychology*, eds. Donald K. Freedheim and Irving B. Weiner (Hoboken, NJ: John Wiley & Sons), 155–76; Louise Leon Thurstone and Thelma Gwinn Thurstone, *Factorial Studies of Intelligence*, Psychometric Monographs Series, no. 2 (Chicago: University of Chicago Press, 1941).

76   Philip Vernon et al., "A Behavioral Genetic Study of Trait Emotional Intelligence," *Emotion* 8, no. 5 (2008): 635–42.

77   See, for instance, Peter D. Harms and Marcus Credé, "Emotional Intelligence and Transformational and Transactional Leadership: A Meta-Analysis," *Journal of Leadership & Organizational Studies* 17 (2010): 5–17.

78   For examples, see Chao Miao, Ronald H. Humphrey, and Shanshan Qian, "Leader Emotional Intelligence and Subordinate Job Satisfaction: A Meta-Analysis of Main, Mediator, and Moderator Effects," *Personality and Individual Differences* 102 (2016): 13–24; Harms and Credé, "Emotional Intelligence"; Ernest H. O'Boyle et al., "The Relation Between Emotional Intelligence and Job Performance: A Meta-Analysis," *Journal of Organizational Behavior* 32, no. 5 (2010): 788–818; A. B. Siegling, Charlotte Nielsen, and K. V. Petrides, "Trait Emotional Intelligence and Leadership in a European Multinational Company," *Personality and Individual Differences* 65 (2014): 65–8.

79   As one such criticism, see Flavia Cavazotte, Valter Moreno, and Mateus Hickmann, "Effects of Leader Intelligence, Personality, and Emotional Intelligence on Transformational Leadership and Managerial Performance," *The Leadership Quarterly* 23 (2012): 443–55.

80   For examples, see Siegling, Nielsen, and Petrides, "Trait Emotional Intelligence"; O'Boyle et al., "Relation."

81   See Dana L. Joseph and Daniel A. Newman, "Emotional Intelligence: An Integrative Meta-Analysis and Cascading Model," *Journal of Applied Psychology* 95 (2010): 54–78.

82   For research supporting this common view, see Christopher Hertzog and K. Warner Schaie, "Stability and Change in Adult Intelligence: I. Analysis of Longitudinal Covariance Structures," *Psychology and Aging* 1, no. 2 (1986): 159–71.

83   Mattingly and Kraiger, "Emotional Intelligence."

84   Reuven Bar-On, "The Bar-On Emotional Quotient Inventory (EQ-i): Rationale, Description and Psychometric Properties," in *Measuring Emotional Intelligence: Common Ground and Controversy*, ed. Glenn Geher (Hauppauge, NY: Nova Science, 2004).

85   David Dunning, "The Dunning-Kruger Effect: On Being Ignorant of One's Own Ignorance," in *Advances in Experimental Social Psychology*, vol. 44, eds. James Olson and Mark P. Zanna (New York: Elsevier, 2011), 247–96.

86   Marshall Goldsmith, "The Most Important Thing You Can Do If You Really Want to Change," *Huffington Post*, March 22, 2015, https://www.huffingtonpost.com/marshall-goldsmith/the-most-important-thing-you-can-do-if-you-really-want-change_b_6509380.html.

87   James M. Kouzes and Barry Z. Posner, *Learning Leadership: The Five Fundamentals of Becoming an Exemplary Leader* (Hoboken, NJ: John Wiley & Sons, 2016).

88   Eunjin Seo et al., "The Effects of Goal Origins and Implementation Intentions on Goal Commitment, Effort, and Performance," *Journal of Experimental Education* 86, no. 3 (2017): 386–401.

89   Nathan W. Hudson et al., "You Have to Follow Through: Attaining Behavioral Change Goals Predicts Volitional Personality Change," *Journal of Personality and Social Psychology* 117, no. 4 (2019): 839–57.

90   Hudson et al., "Follow Through."

91   E. Tory Higgins, "Self-Discrepancy: A Theory Relating Self and Affect," *Psychological Review* 94, no. 3 (1987): 319–40.

92   Chip Heath and Dan Heath, *Switch: How to Change Things When Change Is Hard* (New York: Broadway Books, 2010).

93   Jonathan Haidt, *The Happiness Hypothesis: Finding Modern Truth in Ancient Wisdom* (New York: Basic Books, 2006).

94   Heath and Heath, *Switch*.

95   Heath and Heath, *Switch*, 76.

96   For an application of Kegan's notion of the socialized mind to the context of coaching, see the transcribed interview with Kegan in Tatiana Bachkirova, "Cognitive-Developmental Approach to Coaching: An Interview with Robert Kegan," *Coaching: An International Journal of Theory, Research and Practice* 2 (2009): 10–22.

97   John Doerr, *Measure What Matters: How Google, Bono, and the Gates Foundation Rock the World with OKRs* (New York: Portfolio/Penguin, 2018).

98   Kouzes and Posner, *Learning Leadership*.

99   "Leadership Competencies," Society for Human Resource Management, March 1, 2008, https://www.shrm.org/resourcesandtools/hr-topics/behavioral-competencies/leadership-and-navigation/pages/leadershipcompetencies.aspx.

100   Michael M. Lombardo and Robert W. Eichinger, *FYI: For Your Improvement: A Guide for Development and Coaching* (Minneapolis: Lominger International, 2009).

101   Korn Ferry, *FYI® For Your Improvement: Competencies Development Guide: 38 Global Competency Framework, the Korn Ferry Leadership Architect™*, 2014–2015, https://kpcompetencies.humancontacthosting.com/wp-content/uploads/2019/08/KF-FYI-for-your-improvement-license-ENG-3-4-15.pdf.

102   Korn Ferry, *Compentencies Development*, 5.

103   Bob Kaplan and Rob Kaiser, *The Versatile Leader: Make the Most of Your Strengths—Without Overdoing It* (San Francisco: John Wiley & Sons, 2006).

104   World Economic Forum, *Annual Meeting of the New Champions 2017: Achieving Inclusive Growth in the Fourth Industrial Revolution*, http://www3.weforum.org/docs/AMNC17/WEF_AMNC17_Report.pdf.

105   Thomas A. Kolditz, Tomas Casas i Klett, and John Strackhouse, "Are You a Leader of the Fourth Industrial Revolution?" World Economic Forum, *Annual Meeting of the New Champions 2017: Achieving Inclusive Growth in the Fourth Industrial Revolution*, 40–1, http://www3.weforum.org/docs/AMNC17/WEF_AMNC17_Report.pdf.

106   Judi Brownell, "Meeting the Competency Needs of Global Leaders: A Partnership Approach," Cornell University, School of Hotel Administration, accessed January 26, 2019, https://scholarship.sha.cornell.edu/articles/1082.

107   Troy V. Mumford, Michael A. Campion, and Frederick P. Morgeson, "The Leadership Skills Strataplex: Leadership Skill Requirements Across Organizational Levels," *The Leadership Quarterly* 18, no. 2 (2007): 154–66.

108   For a perspective on the ill-defined terrain of competency definition and measurement across organizations, see Thomas N. Garavan and David Mcguire, "Competencies and Workplace Learning: Some Reflections on the Rhetoric and the Reality," *Journal of Workplace Learning* 13, no. 4 (July 2001): 144–64.

109   For a similar argument, see Benjamin Bloom, *Developing Talent in Young People* (New York: Ballantine Books, 1985).

110   John Doerr, *Measure What Matters: How Google, Bono, and the Gates Foundation Rock the World with OKRs* (New York: Portfolio/Penguin, 2018).

111   Keri Bennington and Tony Laffoley, "Beyond Smiley Sheets: Measuring the ROI of Learning and Development," UNC Kenan-Flagler Business School, 2012, accessed February 14, 2019, http://publicservicesalliance.org/wp-content/uploads/2013/01/Beyond_Smiley_Sheets_-_A_UNC_Executive_Development_White_Paper.pdf.

112   Robert Gandossy and Robin Guarnieri, "Can You Measure Leadership?" *MIT Sloan Management Review* 50, no. 1 (2008): 65–9.

113   Larry Clark, "Measuring the Impact of Leadership Development: Getting Back to Basics," Harvard Business, September 4, 2018, https://www.harvardbusiness.org/measuring-the-impact-of-leadership-development-getting-back-to-basics/.

114   Gandossy and Guarnieri, "Measure Leadership?"

115   Harvard Business School, *2018 State of Leadership Development: Meeting the Transformation Imperative*, accessed February 14, 2019, https://2uzkee3eob510v4rszskfx11-wpengine.netdna-ssl.com/wp-content/uploads/2018/11/20853_CL_StateOfLeadership_Report_2018_Nov2018.pdf.

116   William Shadish, Thomas Cook, and Donald T. Campbell, *Experimental and Quasi-Experimental Designs for Generalized Causal Inference* (Boston, MA: Houghton Mifflin, 2002).

117   Robert R. Haccoun and Thierry Hamtiaux, "Optimizing Knowledge Tests for Inferring Learning Acquisition Levels in Single Group Training Evaluation Designs: The Internal Referencing Strategy," *Personnel Psychology* 47, no. 3 (1994): 593–604.

118   Ryan P. Brown and Lebena Varghese, "Holding Higher Education to Account: Measuring What Matters in the Development of Students as Leaders," *Journal of Character and Leadership Development* 6, no. 2 (2019): 33–48.

119   Michael F. Steger et al., "The Meaning in Life Questionnaire: Assessing the Presence of and Search for Meaning in Life," *Journal of Counseling Psychology* 53, no. 1 (2006): 80–93.

120   E. D. Diener et al., "The Satisfaction with Life Scale," *Journal of Personality Assessment* 49 (1985): 71–5.

121   Kurt Kroenke et al., "An Ultra-Brief Screening Scale for Anxiety and Depression: The PHQ-4," *Psychosomatics* 50, no. 6 (2009): 613–21.

122   Jennifer D. Campbell et al., "Self-Concept Clarity: Measurement, Personality Correlates, and Cultural Boundaries," *Journal of Personality and Social Psychology* 70, no. 1 (1996): 141–56.

123   Ryan P. Brown et al., "Comparing Professional Leadership Coaching Outcomes to Outcomes from Online, Self-Guided Reflection," (white paper, The Doerr Institute for New Leaders, Rice University, Houston, 2020).

124   Ryan P. Brown et al., "The Impact of Professional Coaching on Emerging Leaders" (manuscript under review, 2020).

125   The measure of assertiveness is adapted slightly from Thomas A. Wills, Eli Baker, and Gilbert J. Botvin, "Dimensions of Assertiveness: Differential Relationships to Substance Use in Early Adolescence," *Journal of Consulting and Clinical Psychology*, 57, no. 4 (1989): 473–78; the measure of social self-confidence was adapted from the Texas Social Behavior Inventory, Robert Helmreich and Joy Stapp, "Short Forms of the Texas Social Behavior Inventory (TSBI), An Objective Measure of Self-Esteem," *Bulletin of the Psychonomic Society* 4, no. 5 (1974): 473–5; the measure of rejection sensitivity was from Geraldine Downey and Scott I. Feldman, "Implications of Rejection Sensitivity for Intimate Relationships," *Journal of Personality and Social Psychology* 70, no. 6 (1996): 1327–43.

126   The measure of self-concept clarity is from Campbell et al., "Self-Concept Clarity"; the measure of perfectionistic thoughts and feelings is from Gordon L. Flett et al., "Psychological Distress and the Frequency of Perfectionistic Thinking," *Journal of Personality and Social Psychology* 75, no. 5 (1998): 1363–81; the measure of willingness to delegate is from Janet T. Spence and Anne S. Robbins, "Workaholism: Definition, Measurement, and Preliminary Results," *Journal of Personality Assessment* 58, no. 1 (1992): 160–78.

127   The measures for conflict management come from Carston K. W. De Dreu et al., "A Theory-Based Measure of Conflict Management Strategies in the Workplace," *Journal of Organizational Behavior* 22, no. 6 (2001): 645–68.

128   See David V. Day, Michelle M. Harrison, Stanley M. Halpin, *An Integrative Approach to Leader Development: Connecting Adult Development, Identity, and Expertise* (New York: Taylor & Francis, 2009).

129   Damon Centola et al. "Experimental Evidence for Tipping Points in Social Convention," *Science* 360 (2018): 1116–19.

130   David Noonan, "The 25% Revolution—How Big Does a Minority Have to Be to Reshape Society?" *Scientific American*, June 08, 2018, https://www.scientificamerican.com/article/the-25-revolution-how-big-does-a-minority-have-to-be-to-reshape-society/.

131   Noonan, "25% Revolution."

132   For example, see research by Stéphane Côté et al., "Emotional Intelligence and Leadership Emergence in Small Groups," *The Leadership Quarterly* 21 (2010): 496–508; Ting Hong, Victor M. Catano, and Hui Liao, "Leader Emergence: The Role of Emotional Intelligence and Motivation to Lead," *Leadership & Organizational Development Journal* 32 (2011): 320–43.

133   Michael M. Lombardo and Robert W. Eichinger, *FYI: For Your Improvement: A Guide for Development and Coaching* (Minneapolis: Lominger International, 2009).

134   Christina N. Lacerenza et al., "Leadership Training Design, Delivery, and Implementation: A Meta-Analysis," *Journal of Applied Psychology* 102, no. 12 (2017): 1686–718.

135   Edward L. Thorndike, *Educational Psychology vol. 3: Mental Work and Fatigue and Individual Differences and Their Causes* (New York: Teachers College, 1914).

136   United States Military Academy, *Developing Leaders of Character: West Point Leader Development System 2018 West Point* (New York: United States Military Academy West Point, 2018), 5.

137   Robert Kegan, *The Evolving Self: Problem and Process in Human Development* (Cambridge, MA: Harvard University Press, 1982).

138   Robert J. Sternberg et al., *Practical Intelligence in Everyday Life* (New York: Cambridge University Press, 2000).

139   Robert Caslen, Jr. and Michael Matthews, *The Character Edge: Leading and Winning With Integrity* (New York: St. Martin's Press, 2020).

140   James J. Connors, Jonathan J. Velez, and Benjamin G. Swan, "Leadership Characteristics of Outstanding Seniors in a Land-Grant University College of Agriculture," *Journal of Leadership Education* 5, no. 3 (2006): 93–126.

141   Thomas Kolditz, "New Leader Development: Leadership Lessons from the Doerr Institute," in *Work Is Love Made Visible: A Collection of Essays about the Power of Finding Your Purpose from the World's Greatest Thought Leaders*, eds. Francis Hesselbein, Marshall Goldsmith, and Sarah McArthur (Hoboken, NJ: John Wiley & Sons, 2019), 188–9.

142   See "Mission and Values," Rice University, accessed January 26, 2019 https://www.rice.edu/mission-values.

143   Lombardo and Eichinger, *FYI*.

Bibliography

Almond, B. J. "Ann and John Doerr Donate $50M to Develop New Leaders at Rice." Rice News. May 14, 2015. http://news.rice.edu/2015/05/14/ann-and-john-doerr-donate-50m-to-develop-new-leaders-at-rice-university.

Arnett, Jeffrey Jensen. "Emerging Adulthood: A Theory of Development from the Late Teens Through the Twenties." *American Psychologist* 55, no. 5 (2000): 469–80.

Arvey, Richard, Zhen Zhang, Bruce J. Avolio, and Robert F. Krueger. "Developmental and Genetic Determinants of Leadership Role Occupancy in Women." *Journal of Applied Psychology* 92, no. 3 (2007): 693–706.

Avolio, Bruce J., and Gretchen R. Vogelgesang. "Beginnings Matter in Genuine Leadership Development." In *Early Development and Leadership: Building the Next Generation of Leaders*, edited by Susan Elaine Murphy and Rebecca J. Reichard, 179–204. New York: Taylor & Francis, 2011.

Bachkirova, Tatiana. "Cognitive-Developmental Approach to Coaching: An Interview with Robert Kegan." *Coaching: An International Journal of Theory, Research and Practice* 2 (2009): 10–22.

Bar-On, Reuven. "The Bar-On Emotional Quotient Inventory (EQ-i): Rationale, Description and Psychometric Properties." In *Measuring Emotional Intelligence: Common Ground and Controversy*, edited by Glenn Geher. Hauppauge, NY: Nova Science, 2004.

Bennington, Keri, and Tony Laffoley. "Beyond Smiley Sheets: Measuring the ROI of Learning and Development." UNC Kenan-Flagler Business School, 2012. Accessed February 14, 2019. http://public-servicesalliance.org/wp-content/uploads/2013/01/Beyond_Smiley_Sheets_-_A_UNC_Executive_Development_White_Paper.pdf.

Bloom, Benjamin. *Developing Talent in Young People*. New York: Ballantine Books, 1985.

Bono, Joyce E., and Timothy A. Judge. "Personality and Transformational and Transactional Leadership: A Meta-Analysis." *Journal of Applied Psychology* 89, no. 5 (2004): 901–10.

Brown, Ryan P., and Eric Anthony Day. "The Difference Isn't Black and White: Stereotype Threat and the Race Gap on Raven's Advanced Progressive Matrices." *Journal of Applied Psychology* 91, no. 4 (2006): 979–85.

Brown, Ryan P., and Lebena Varghese. "Holding Higher Education to Account: Measuring What Matters in the Development of Students as Leaders." *Journal of Character and Leadership Development* 6, no. 2 (2019): 33–48.

Brown, Ryan P., Lebena Varghese, Sarah Sullivan, and Sandra Parsons. "Comparing Professional Leadership Coaching Outcomes to Outcomes from Online, Self-Guided Reflection." White Paper, The Doerr Institute for New Leaders, Rice University, Houston, 2020.

Brown, Ryan P., Lebena Varghese, Sarah Sullivan, and Sandra Parsons. "The Impact of Professional Coaching on Emerging Leaders." Manuscript Under Review, 2020.

Brownell, Judi. "Meeting the Competency Needs of Global Leaders: A Partnership Approach." Cornell University, School of Hotel Administration. Accessed January 26, 2019. https://scholarship.sha.cornell.edu/articles/1082.

Burt, Cyril. "The Genetic Determination of Differences in Intelligence: A Study of Monozygotic Twins Reared Together and Apart." *British Journal of Psychology* 57, no. 1-2 (1966): 137–53.

Burt, Daniel, and Zenobia Talati. "The Unsolved Value of Executive Coaching: A Meta-Analysis of Outcomes Using Randomized Control Trial Studies." *International Journal of Evidence Based Coaching and Mentoring* 15, no. 2 (2017): 17–24.

Burton, Tara Isabella. "Why Are American Colleges Obsessed With 'Leadership'?" *The Atlantic.* January 22, 2014. https://www.the-atlantic.com/education/archive/2014/01/why-are-american-colleges-obsessed-with-leadership/283253.

Byrne, John. "How Much Attention Should You Pay to U.S. News' College Rankings?" *Forbes*. September 10, 2018. https://www.forbes.com/sites/poetsandquants/2018/09/10/how-much-attention-should-you-pay-to-u-s-news-college-rankings/#1bb3f257daf7.

Campbell, Jennifer D., Paul D. Trapnell, Steven J. Heine, Ilana M. Katz, Loraine F. Lavallee, and Darrin R. Lehman. "Self-Concept Clarity: Measurement, Personality Correlates, and Cultural Boundaries." *Journal of Personality and Social Psychology* 70, no. 1 (1996): 141–56.

Caslen, Robert, Jr., and Michael Matthews. *The Character Edge: Leading and Winning With Integrity*. New York: St. Martin's Press, 2020.

Cavazotte, Flavia, Valter Moreno, and Mateus Hickmann. "Effects of Leader Intelligence, Personality, and Emotional Intelligence on Transformational Leadership and Managerial Performance." *The Leadership Quarterly* 23 (2012): 443–55.

Centola, Damon, Joshua Becker, Devon Brackbill, and Andrea Baronshelli. "Experimental Evidence for Tipping Points in Social Convention." *Science* 360 (2018): 1116–19.

Clark, Larry. "Measuring the Impact of Leadership Development: Getting Back to Basics." Harvard Business. September 4, 2018. https://www.harvardbusiness.org/measuring-the-impact-of-leadership-development-getting-back-to-basics.

Collins, Jim. *Good to Great: Why Some Companies Make the Leap...and Others Don't*. New York: HarperBusiness, 2001.

Collins, Jim. *Good to Great and the Social Sectors: Why Business Thinking Is Not the Answer*. New York: HarperCollins, 2005.

Connors, James J., Jonathan J. Velez, and Benjamin G. Swan. "Leadership Characteristics of Outstanding Seniors in a Land-Grant University College of Agriculture." *Journal of Leadership Education* 5, no. 3 (2006): 93–126.

Côté, Stéphane, Paulo N. Lopes, Peter Salovey, Christopher T. H. Miners. "Emotional Intelligence and Leadership Emergence in Small Groups." *The Leadership Quarterly* 21 (2010): 496–508.

Cousins, Sophie. "Measles: A Global Resurgence." *The Lancet* 19, no. 4 (2019): 362–3.

Day, David V., Michelle M. Harrison, Stanley M. Halpin. *An Integrative Approach to Leader Development: Connecting Adult Development, Identity, and Expertise.* New York: Taylor & Francis, 2009.

De Dreu, Carston K. W., Arne Evers, Bianca Beersma, Esther S. Kluwer, and Aukje Nauta. "A Theory-Based Measure of Conflict Management Strategies in the Workplace." *Journal of Organizational Behavior* 22, no. 6 (2001): 645–68.

Diener, E. D., Robert A. Emmons, Randy J. Larsen, and Sharon Griffin. "The Satisfaction with Life Scale." *Journal of Personality Assessment* 49 (1985): 71–5.

Doerr, John. *Measure What Matters: How Google, Bono, and the Gates Foundation Rock the World with OKRs.* New York: Portfolio/Penguin, 2018.

Downey, Geraldine, and Scott I. Feldman. "Implications of Rejection Sensitivity for Intimate Relationships." *Journal of Personality and Social Psychology* 70, no. 6 (1996): 1327–43.

Dunlop, Connie Whittaker, and Forbes Coaches Council. "The Success and Failure of the Coaching Industry." *Forbes.* October 5, 2017. https://www.forbes.com/sites/forbescoachescouncil/2017/10/05/the-success-and-failure-of-the-coaching-industry/#3aa42c666765.

Dunning, David. "The Dunning-Kruger Effect: On Being Ignorant of One's Own Ignorance." In *Advances in Experimental Social Psychology*, vol. 44, edited by James Olson and Mark P. Zanna, 247–96. New York: Elsevier, 2011.

Edelman. "2018 Edelman TRUST BAROMETER." January 21, 2018. https://www.edelman.com/research/2018-edelman-trust-barometer.

Ely, Katherine, Lisa A. Boyce, Jonathan K. Nelson, Steven J. Zaccaro, Gina Hernez-Broome, and Wynne Whyman. "Evaluating Leadership Coaching: A Review and Integrated Framework." *The Leadership Quarterly* 21 (2010): 585–99.

Erlenmeyer-Kimling, Loise, and Lissy F. Jarvik. "Genetics and Intelligence: A Review." *Science* 142, no. 3598 (1963): 1477–79.

Flett, Gordon L., Paul L. Hewitt, Kirk R. Blankstein, and Lisa Gray. "Psychological Distress and the Frequency of Perfectionistic Thinking." *Journal of Personality and Social Psychology 75, no.* 5 (1998): 1363–81.

Forbes Coaches Council. "15 Trends That Will Redefine Executive Coaching in the Next Decade." *Forbes.* April 9, 2018. https://www.forbes.com/sites/forbescoachescouncil/2018/04/09/15-trends-that-will-redefine-executive-coaching-in-the-next-decade/#76b5911d6fc9.

Funk, Cary. "Mixed Messages about Public Trust in Science." Pew Research Center Science & Society, August 27, 2020. https://www.pewresearch.org/science/2017/12/08/mixed-messages-about-public-trust-in-science.

Funk, Cary, Meg Hefferon, Brian Kennedy, and Courtney Johnson. "Americans Generally View Medical Professionals Favorably, but About Half Consider Misconduct a Big Problem." Pew Research Center Science & Society, August 2, 2019, https://www.pewresearch.org/science/2019/08/02/americans-generally-view-medical-professionals-favorably-but-about-half-consider-misconduct-a-big-problem.

Gandossy, Robert, and Robin Guarnieri. "Can You Measure Leadership?" *MIT Sloan Management Review* 50, no. 1 (2008): 65–9.

Garavan, Thomas N., and David Mcguire. "Competencies and Workplace Learning: Some Reflections on the Rhetoric and the Reality." *Journal of Workplace Learning* 13, no. 4 (July 2001): 144–64.

Goldsmith, Marshall. "The Most Important Thing You Can Do If You Really Want to Change." *Huffington Post*, March 22, 2015. https://www.huffingtonpost.com/marshall-goldsmith/the-most-important-thing-you-can-do-if-you-really-want-change_b_6509380.html.

Goleman, Daniel. *"Emotional Intelligence: Why It Can Matter More Than IQ.* New York: Bantam Books, 1995.

GoodReads. "William Faulkner Quotes." Accessed January 7, 2019. https://www.goodreads.com/quotes/79715-in-writing-you-must-kill-all-your-darlings.

Grant, Anthony M., Linley Curtayne, and Geraldine Burton. "Executive Coaching Enhances Goal Attainment, Resilience and Workplace Well-Being: A Randomised Controlled Study." *The Journal of Positive Psychology* 4, no. 5 (2009): 396–407.

Haccoun, Robert R., and Thierry Hamtiaux. "Optimizing Knowledge Tests for Inferring Learning Acquisition Levels in Single Group Training Evaluation Designs: The Internal Referencing Strategy." *Personnel Psychology* 47, no. 3 (1994): 593–604.

Haidt, Jonathan. *The Happiness Hypothesis: Finding Modern Truth in Ancient Wisdom*. New York: Basic Books, 2006.

Harms, Peter D., and Marcus Credé. "Emotional Intelligence and Transformational and Transactional Leadership: A Meta-Analysis." *Journal of Leadership & Organizational Studies* 17 (2010): 5–17.

Harrell, Melissa, and Lauren Barbato. "Great Managers Still Matter: The Evolution of Google's Project Oxygen." February 27, 2018. https://rework.withgoogle.com/blog/the-evolution-of-project-oxygen.

Harrington, Matthew. "For the First Time in 17 Years, People's Trust Declined in Every Kind of Institution We Asked About." Harvard Business Review, April 11, 2017. https://hbr.org/2017/01/survey-peoples-trust-has-declined-in-business-media-government-and-ngos.

Harvard Business School. *2018 State of Leadership Development: Meeting the Transformation Imperative*. Accessed February 14, 2019. https://www.harvardbusiness.org/insight/the-state-of-leadership-development-report.

Heath, Chip, and Dan Heath. *Switch: How to Change Things When Change Is Hard*. New York: Broadway Books, 2010.

Helmreich, Robert, and Joy Stapp. "Short Forms of the Texas Social Behavior Inventory (TSBI), An Objective Measure of Self-Esteem." *Bulletin of the Psychonomic Society* 4, no. 5 (1974): 473–5.

Hertzog, Christopher, and K. Warner Schaie. "Stability and Change in Adult Intelligence: I. Analysis of Longitudinal Covariance Structures." *Psychology and Aging* 1, no. 2 (1986): 159–71.

Higgins, E. Tory. "Self-Discrepancy: A Theory Relating Self and Affect." *Psychological Review* 94, no. 3 (1987): 319–40.

Hiller, Nathan J. "An Examination of Leadership Beliefs and Leadership Self-Identity: Constructs, Correlates, and Outcomes." PhD diss., The Pennsylvania State University, 2005.

Hong, Ting, Victor M. Catano, and Hui Liao. "Leader Emergence: The Role of Emotional Intelligence and Motivation to Lead." *Leadership & Organizational Development Journal* 32 (2011): 320–43.

Hudson, Nathan W., Daniel A. Briley, William J. Chopik, and Jamie Derringer. "You Have to Follow Through: Attaining Behavioral Change Goals Predicts Volitional Personality Change." *Journal of Personality and Social Psychology* 117, no. 4 (2019): 839–57.

Ibarra, Herminia. *Act Like a Leader, Think Like a Leader*. Boston: HBR Press, 2015.

International Coach Federation. "About ICF." Accessed August 21, 2020. https://coachfederation.org/about.

International Coach Federation. "Credential Updates." Accessed August 21, 2020. https://coachfederation.org/credential-updates.

International Coach Federation Houston Charter Chapter. "Types of Coaching." Accessed August 21, 2020. https://icfhoustoncoaches.org/Types_of_Coaching.

Jabr, Ferris. "The Neuroscience of 20-Somethings." *Scientific American*, August 29, 2012. https://blogs.scientificamerican.com/brainwaves/the-neuroscience-of-twenty-somethings.

Jaschik, Scott. "Oklahoma Gave False Data for Years to 'U.S. News,' Loses Ranking." *Inside Higher Ed*, May 28, 2019. https://www.insidehighered.com/admissions/article/2019/05/28/university-oklahoma-stripped-us-news-ranking-supplying-false.

Johnson, Sara B., Robert W. Blum, and Jay N. Giedd. "Adolescent Maturity and the Brain: The Promise and Pitfalls of Neuroscience Research in Adolescent Health Policy." *Journal of Adolescent Health* 45, no. 3 (September 2009): 216–21. https://www.ncbi.nlm.nih.gov/pmc/articles/PMC2892678.

Jones, Rebecca, Steven A. Woods, and Yves R. Guillaume. "The Effectiveness of Workplace Coaching: A Meta-Analysis of Learning and Performance Outcomes from Coaching." *Journal of Occupational and Organizational Psychology* 89, no. 2 (2016): 249–77.

Joseph, Dana L., and Daniel A. Newman. "Emotional Intelligence: An Integrative Meta-Analysis and Cascading Model." *Journal of Applied Psychology* 95 (2010): 54–78.

Kaiser, Robert B., and Gordy Curphy. "Leadership Development: The Failure of an Industry and the Opportunity for Consulting Psychologists." *Consulting Psychology Journal: Practice and Research* 65, no. 4 (2013): 294–302.

Kaplan, Bob, and Rob Kaiser. *The Versatile Leader: Make the Most of Your Strengths—Without Overdoing It*. San Francisco: John Wiley & Sons, 2006.

Kegan, Robert. *The Evolving Self: Problem and Process in Human Development*. Cambridge, MA: Harvard University Press, 1982.

Kolditz, Thomas. "New Leader Development: Leadership Lessons from the Doerr Institute." In *Work Is Love Made Visible: A Collection of Essays about the Power of Finding Your Purpose from the World's Greatest Thought Leaders*, edited by Francis Hesselbein, Marshall Goldsmith, and Sarah McArthur, 188–9. Hoboken, NJ: John Wiley & Sons, 2019.

Kolditz, Thomas A., Tomas Casas i Klett, and John Strackhouse. "Are You a Leader of the Fourth Industrial Revolution?" World Economic Forum, Annual Meeting of the New Champions 2017: Achieving Inclusive Growth in the Fourth Industrial Revolution, 40–1. http://www3.weforum.org/docs/AMNC17/WEF_AMNC17_Report.pdf.

Korn Ferry, *FYI® For Your Improvement: Competencies Development Guide: 38 Global Competency Framework, the Korn Ferry Leadership Architect™*, 2014–2015. https://kpcompetencies.humancontacthosting.com/wp-content/uploads/2019/08/KF-FYI-for-your-improvement-license-ENG-3-4-15.pdf.

Kouzes, James M., and Barry Z. Posner. *Learning Leadership: The Five Fundamentals of Becoming an Exemplary Leader*. Hoboken, NJ: John Wiley & Sons, 2016.

Kroenke, Kurt, Robert Spitzer, Janet B. Williams, and Bernd Löwe. "An Ultra-Brief Screening Scale for Anxiety and Depression: The PHQ-4." *Psychosomatics* 50, no. 6 (2009): 613–21.

Lacerenza, Christina N., Denise Reyes, Shannon L. Marlow, Dana L. Joseph, and Eduardo Salas. "Leadership Training Design, Delivery, and Implementation: A Meta-Analysis." *Journal of Applied Psychology* 102, no. 12 (2017): 1686–718.

Lombardo, Michael M., and Robert W. Eichinger. *FYI: For Your Improvement: A Guide for Development and Coaching*. Minneapolis: Lominger International, 2009.

Lord, Robert G., David V. Day, Steven J. Zaccaro, Bruce J. Avolio, and Alice H. Eagly. "Leadership in Applied Psychology: Three Waves of Theory and Research." *Journal of Applied Psychology* 102, no. 3 (2017): 434–51.

Lord, Robert G., and Rosalie J. Hall. "Identity, Deep Structure and the Development of Leadership Skill." *The Leadership Quarterly* 16, no. 4 (2005): 591–615.

Mattingly, Victoria, and Kurt Kraiger. "Can Emotional Intelligence Be Trained? A Meta-Analytical Investigation." *Human Resource Management Review* 29, no. 2 (2019): 140–55.

Miao, Chao, Ronald H. Humphrey, and Shanshan Qian. "Leader Emotional Intelligence and Subordinate Job Satisfaction: A Meta-Analysis of Main, Mediator, and Moderator Effects." *Personality and Individual Differences* 102 (2016): 13–24.

Miscenko, Darja, Hannes Guenter, and David V. Day. "Am I a Leader? Examining Leader Development Over Time." *The Leadership Quarterly* 28, no. 5 (2017): 605–20.

Mumford, Troy V., Michael A. Campion, and Frederick P. Morgeson. "The Leadership Skills Strataplex: Leadership Skill Requirements Across Organizational Levels." *The Leadership Quarterly* 18, no. 2 (2007): 154–66.

Neegaard, Lauran, and Hannah Fingerhut. "AP-NORC Poll: Half of Americans Would Get a COVID-19 Vaccine." *Associated Press*, May 27, 2020. https://apnews.com/dacdc8bc428dd4df6511b-fa259cfec44.

Noonan, David. "The 25% Revolution—How Big Does a Minority Have to Be to Reshape Society?" *Scientific American*. June 8, 2018. https://www.scientificamerican.com/article/the-25-revolution-how-big-does-a-minority-have-to-be-to-reshape-society.

NPR. "Our Roaring 20s: 'The Defining Decade.'" April 22, 2012. https://www.npr.org/2012/04/22/150429128/our-roaring-20s-the-defining-decade.

O'Boyle, Ernest H., Ronald H. Humphrey, Jeffrey M. Pollack, Thomas H. Hawver, and Paul A. Story. "The Relation Between Emotional Intelligence and Job Performance: A Meta-Analysis." *Journal of Organizational Behavior* 32, no. 5 (2010): 788–818.

Payne, Sarah. "93% of Managers Need Training on Coaching Employees." Workhuman, March 21, 2017. https://www.workhuman.com/resources/globoforce-blog/survey-93-of-managers-need-training-on-coaching-employees.

Pelaez Arias, Celina. "World Domination: 10 Best Schools for Student Leaders." *College Magazine*, August 18, 2015. https://www.collegemagazine.com/world-domination-cms-top-10-schools-future-leaders.

Rice University. "Mission and Values." Accessed January 26, 2019. https://www.rice.edu/mission-values.

Rice University. "Rice University." Office of Proposal Development. Accessed January 10, 2019. https://opd.rice.edu/boilerplate-materials/rice-university.

Salovey, Peter, and John Mayer. "Emotional Intelligence." *Imagination, Cognition, and Personality* 9, no. 3 (1990): 185–211.

Salthouse, Timothy A. "Mediation of Adult Age Differences in Cognition by Reductions in Working Memory and Speed of Processing." *Psychological Science* 2, no. 3 (1991): 179–83.

Saposky, Robert M. *Behave: The Biology of Humans at Our Best and Worst.* New York: Penguin Books, 2017.

Schein, Edgar H. *Humble Inquiry: The Gentle Art of Asking Instead of Telling.* San Francisco: Berrett-Koehler Publishers, 2013.

Schmidt, Eric, Jonathan Rosenber, and Alan Eagle. *Trillion Dollar Coach: The Leadership Playbook of Silicon Valley's Bill Campbell.* New York: Harper Business, 2019.

Seo, Eunjin, Erika A. Patall, Marlone D. Henderson, and Rebecca R. Steingut. "The Effects of Goal Origins and Implementation Intentions on Goal Commitment, Effort, and Performance." *Journal of Experimental Education* 86, no. 3 (2017): 386–401.

Shadish, William, Thomas Cook, and Donald T. Campbell. *Experimental and Quasi-Experimental Designs for Generalized Causal Inference.* Boston: Houghton Mifflin, 2002.

Sherman, Stratford, and Alyssa Freas. "The Wild West of Executive Coaching." *Harvard Business Review,* November 2004. https://hbr.org/2004/11/the-wild-west-of-executive-coaching.

Siegling, A. B., Charlotte Nielsen, and K. V. Petrides. "Trait Emotional Intelligence and Leadership in a European Multinational Company." *Personality and Individual Differences* 65 (2014): 65–8.

Society for Human Resource Management. "Leadership Competencies." March 1, 2008. https://www.shrm.org/resourcesandtools/hr-topics/behavioral-competencies/leadership-and-navigation/pages/leadershipcompetencies.aspx.

Spence, Janet T., and Anne S. Robbins. "Workaholism: Definition, Measurement, and Preliminary Results." *Journal of Personality Assessment* 58, no. 1 (1992): 160–78.

Srivastava, Sanjay, Oliver P. John, Samual D. Gosling, and Jeff Potter. "Development of Personality in Early and Middle Adulthood: Set Like Plaster or Persistent Change?" *Journal of Personality and Social Psychology* 84, no. 5 (2003): 1041–53.

Steger, Michael F., Patricia Frazier, Shigehiro Oishi, and Matthew Kaler. "The Meaning in Life Questionnaire: Assessing the Presence of and Search for Meaning in Life." *Journal of Counseling Psychology* 53, no. 1 (2006): 80–93.

Sternberg, Robert J. "Intelligence." In *Handbook of Psychology: History of Psychology*, edited by Donald K. Freedheim and Irving B. Weiner, 155–76. Hoboken, NJ: John Wiley & Sons.

Sternberg, Robert J., George B. Forsythe, Jennifer Hedlund, Richard K. Wagner, Joseph A. Horvath, Wendy M. Williams, Scott A. Snook, and Elena Grigorenko. *Practical Intelligence in Everyday Life*. New York: Cambridge University Press, 2000.

Thorndike, Edward L. *Educational Psychology vol. 3: Mental Work and Fatigue and Individual Differences and Their Causes*. New York: Teachers College, 1914.

Thornton, George C., and William Byham. *Assessment Centers and Managerial Performance*. New York: Academic Press, 1982.

Thurstone, Louise Leon, and Thelma Gwinn Thurstone. *Factorial Studies of Intelligence*. Psychometric Monographs Series, no. 2. Chicago: University of Chicago Press, 1941.

U.S. News Staff. "2019 Best Colleges Preview: Top 25 National Universities." *U.S. News & World Report*, September 7, 2018. https://www.usnews.com/education/best-colleges/articles/2018-09-07/2019-best-colleges-preview-top-25-national-universities.

United States Military Academy, *Developing Leaders of Character: West Point Leader Development System 2018 West Point*. New York: United States Military Academy West Point, 2018.

Vernon, Philip, K. V. Petrides, Denis Bratko, and Julie A. Schermer. "A Behavioral Genetic Study of Trait Emotional Intelligence." *Emotion* 8, no. 5 (2008): 635–42.

Wai, Jonathan, and Heiner Rindermann. "What Goes Into High Educational and Occupational Achievement? Education, Brains, Hard Work, Networks, and Other Factors." *High Ability Studies* 28 (2017): 127–45.

Wills, Thomas A., Eli Baker, and Gilbert J. Botvin. "Dimensions of Assertiveness: Differential Relationships to Substance Use in Early Adolescence." *Journal of Consulting and Clinical Psychology 57*, no. 4 (1989): 473–78

World Economic Forum. *Annual Meeting of the New Champions 2017: Achieving Inclusive Growth in the Fourth Industrial Revolution.* http://www3.weforum.org/docs/AMNC17/WEF_AMNC17_Report.pdf.

Yale College. "What Yale Looks For." Yale College Undergraduate Admissions. Accessed January 9, 2019. https://admissions.yale.edu/what-yale-looks-for.

Yeager, Katherine L., and Jamie L. Callahan. "Learning to Lead: Foundations of Emerging Leader Identity Development." *Advances in Developing Human Resources* 18, no. 3 (2016): 286–300.